REAL MADRID CF
SL BENFICA
C INTERNAZIONALE MILANO
CELTIC FC
FEYENOORD
AFC AJAX
FC BAYERN MUNCHEN
NOTTINGHAM FOREST FC
ASTON VILLA FC
JUVENTUS
PSV EINDHOVEN
FK CRVENA ZVEZDA
AC MILAN
BORUSSIA DORTMUND
REAL MADRID CF
AC MILAN
FC BARCELONA

FC BARCELONA
MADRID CF

OLIVIER
GIROUD

OLIVIER
GIROUD

Always Believe

First published by Pitch Publishing, 2021

Pitch Publishing
A2 Yeoman Gate
Yeoman Way
Worthing
Sussex
BN13 3QZ
www.pitchpublishing.co.uk
info@pitchpublishing.co.uk

A CIP catalogue record is available for this book
from the British Library.

ISBN: 978-1-80150-009-8

Typesetting and origination by Pitch Publishing
Printed and bound in Great Britain by TJ Books, Padstow

Contents

To Jade, Evan, Aaron and Aria

Preface

I DON'T like talking about myself. I'm modest and discreet, and I've always been reluctant to open up too much about my life and put my family on show. And anyway, I'm only 34. It's fair to say you don't publish your autobiography at that age. The idea that I might write something wasn't at the forefront of my mind, but all the same it was gnawing away at me in the background. In June 2019, a phone call got the ball rolling. I hadn't approached anyone about it, but there we were, it was being suggested that I write a book.

Was it the right time? Shouldn't I wait until the end of my career? I thought about it long and hard, but I'm a great believer in fate. I also believe that chance encounters never actually happen by chance. I agreed to tell my story.

Writing this book has led me to look back at my past from different angles. I've made time to sit down and really take stock, to evaluate the path my life has taken. I talk about the subjects close to my heart: my faith, my family and my success, of course; as well as the moments of doubt, and the setbacks I've had to overcome to get to where I am today. There is no subject I've avoided writing about. In these pages, I reveal myself as I've never dared do before. Candidly and openly. The plain, unvarnished truth.

I became a footballer out of passion, mostly, but also to make my loved ones proud. That hunger for recognition makes me wonder where this need to be the centre of attention comes from. On the pitch, I'm neither a defender nor a midfielder, I'm a striker. A player who scores goals, who gets the crowd out of their seats and on their feet. Who shows off on the pitch, dazzles millions of people and, with one skilful manoeuvre or a spectacular piece of play, can secure victory for his team. We'll come back to this point about standing out from the crowd.

More than other people, probably, I have a need to be in the limelight. The circumstances surrounding my conception and birth are not unconnected to this desire to simply show the world that I exist. My birth – which I'll talk about at length later in the book – is like a fault line on which I built the mental strength that has allowed me to overcome every obstacle in my path. My birth made me the man I am today: sensitive, hungry for success, squeezing the most out of every minute of his existence, driven by a furious desire to live.

My book is for athletes and footballers, but more broadly – and especially – for everyone out there who doubts themselves, who despairs, who gives up. For everyone who has dreams but never dares make them come true.

To those of you who have resigned yourselves to your fate, I say: just look at me! I've been a world champion – who could have imagined that? Nothing marked me out for this career. I made my dreams come true because I believed in them and I created my own opportunities. I wanted it badly enough. I fought for it. The strength that my faith in God gives me every day did the rest.

Don't give up. Keep going. Have confidence as well as humility. Believe in yourself and in life. Never let anyone or anything crush your ambitions.

This is an ethos I try to pass on to my children, Jade, Evan, Aaron and Aria. My story is dedicated to them most of all, like a legacy or a message of hope. To tell them that in life, nothing is impossible.

The important thing is to always believe.

1

World Champion

The day of the final

Sunday, 15 July 2018. The World Cup Final. Moscow's Olympic venue, the Luzhniki Stadium, is absolutely packed. The Croats outnumber us three or four to one, but our supporters are out there, noisily making their presence felt. They sing, they cheer us on, they get out of their seats and roar whenever we get anywhere near the opposing goal. It's 28 degrees, the heat is stifling. The sky darkens as the minutes tick by. There's a storm on its way. A heavy atmosphere hangs in the air. Faces are strained and bodies exhausted. What does it matter, though?

We're leading 4-1 against Croatia. If all goes well, in a little over 20 minutes we will be world champions.

The 69th minute. Hugo Lloris shows too much of the ball to Croatian forward Mario Mandžukić, who steals it from him; 4-2! The tension steps up a notch. This goal feeds the hunger to win on both sides. Galvanised by this mistake on our part, our opponents become more threatening. We resist, desperate to win this second victory for the nation, and my first.

The 81st minute. The manager takes me off and brings on the young attacking midfielder, Nabil Fekir. The crowd applauds me, and chants my name, even though I haven't scored a single goal in this tournament. But this is not the time for regrets or reflection. I come off the pitch. As usual, I think of Jesus and look up at the sky for a few moments. This evening in particular, I say a short prayer to ask him to help. At the same time, I'm focused on the match unfolding before me. There are ten minutes of normal time left. I know everything can change from one moment to the next, that no team is safe from a sudden reversal of fortune, but I really am starting to believe we can do it. How can the Croats come back and score with so little time left?

I head to the bench to join my team-mates. I sit down beside them – Adil Rami, Djibril Sidibé, Steve Mandanda and Florian Thauvin. We're jittery as anything. All eyes are on the clock. The minutes drag on. As if to ward off bad luck, I keep repeating the same words over and over again to Florian, who isn't even listening, 'We're going to do it! We're going to do it!' There are just five minutes left to play. My childhood dream is about to come true. My family are just a few metres away in the stands: my wife Jennifer, my daughter Jade, five years old at the time, my parents, my brother Romain, my brother-in-law and the friends I've had since I was a kid. They're counting the seconds. It makes me happy to bring them so much joy. They've always believed in me.

Still 4-2. No change to the score. We go into stoppage time. None of us can sit still a minute longer and we move to the edge of the pitch, standing ready to leap in the air at the sound of the final whistle. I catch sight of the manager. He's calm and focused, but the smile on his face speaks for itself. He's pulled it off and is proud of his team. Tonight he is pushing them onwards to the ultimate prize, just like he had been pushed himself, 20 years ago almost to the day.

The referee blows his whistle. I stop thinking about anything. My mind is a blur and there are no words to describe what I'm feeling. I race on to the pitch, whooping with joy. I throw myself face down inside the opponents' goal. The sky cracks and the first drops of rain begin to fall. Adil Rami rushes at me like a tornado, and we embrace. I barely remember anything of the next few minutes. I'm on another planet, the emotion overwhelming me. I fall into the arms of Thierry Marszalek, a stalwart of the French staff for two decades: his job is to analyse opposing teams. I cry on his shoulder, like a little kid. 'Oli, I'm happy for you, you deserve this cup,' he whispers in my ear.

My tears keep falling. I'm hugging everyone I see. Guy Stéphan, Didier Deschamps' assistant, says to me, 'So, then? We can't be champions with Giroud on the team?' He's talking about the doubts the press have expressed about whether I deserve my place on the team and the criticism I've been on the receiving end of ever since the manager first picked me for the squad. I try not to attach any importance to what journalists write about me. I know that only hard work pays off, so I slog away, I graft, I give it my all. Even if sometimes that isn't enough.

Making the squad

The two seasons leading up to the World Cup are tough. After a good Euro 2016 – despite losing to Portugal in the final – I return to Arsenal, feeling pumped up and strong from my best season for France and my best club season too: 38 goals scored in all competitions. I barely have time to enjoy the moment before I get a shock that hits me like a cold shower. My manager at the time, Arsène Wenger, decides to change his tactics at the start of the season and puts Alexis Sánchez up front. Then, within a year and a half, he signs two forwards, first Alexandre Lacazette, then a little later Pierre-Emerick Aubameyang. I'm upset by this decision, but competition is part of the job and I accept it. I'm ready to fight to earn my place. It's futile. Lacazette scores goals; I stay on the bench.

Every time the French team is called up for international duty, manager Didier Deschamps gives me a warning, 'Oli, you're not getting enough game time. You have to play more, you have to train more so you're in good shape and can get back on the pitch, because nothing can replace the intensity of real matches. If you don't do that, you're unlikely to be on the squad for the World Cup.'

Deschamps trusts me and has always supported me, despite attacks from the media who constantly question my role and how useful I really am to the team. This time, the reality of the situation sinks in. It's a fact that

I don't play enough at Arsenal. To get called up for the national team, we need to play a minimum number of matches. The manager is only doing his duty by giving me this warning. Most of our conversations take place in private. He calls me in to see him and we talk. 'I know how much you've brought to the team, and you still do, but that doesn't give you a free pass.' How could he justify his decision to select me when some of my team-mates are first-choice players for their clubs?

He's right. The pressure is on. I'm quite clear-headed about my situation and, besides, I don't feel ready to compete in an important tournament like this with so little match time under my belt. In January 2018, five months before the World Cup, I decide to leave Arsenal to sign for Chelsea. Finally, I start playing and scoring goals again. Russia is ready and waiting to welcome me.

On 17 May 2018, at 8pm, the names of the 23 players selected for the World Cup squad will be announced on TF1, one of the main TV channels. I'm at home, sitting quietly in front of the telly waiting for

Didier to make his announcement. I'm feeling perfectly relaxed. In fact, I have to admit that I'm not actually dreading this moment at all. I'm in the starting 11 and the head coach chooses 23 players, so it's kind of obvious I'll make the squad.

This might seem strange, but we only learn whether or not we've been selected by watching it on TV. We don't get a heads up from the manager. Ten days or so before the official announcement of which 23 have made the squad, 50 players receive an email at their club informing them they're on the provisional call-up list. For those who aren't certain of being chosen, the suspense is unbearable.

On 23 May, we meet at the Clairefontaine training centre to start our preparations for the World Cup. The squad is already solid and the atmosphere relaxed but focused. The aim is clear: to be ready for the opener against Australia. After a hectic season, I feel physically tired, but the staff have fine-tuned a tailor-made programme so that we're at the top of our game come D-Day. Mentally, I'm fine. I have no idea of the challenges that lie ahead.

Welcome to Russia

A week before the first round of the competition, we're playing a friendly in Lyon against the USA. I come into an aerial challenge with defender Matt Miazga too late and my head clashes hard with his. Blood streaming down my face, I fall to the ground and stay there, completely out of it. I fear the worst, but the medics reassure me that I've taken the hit above my browbone and that's why I'm bleeding so much. In shock, I exit the pitch with a bandage round my head. Six stitches for me, 15 for Matt.

The next day, we fly off for our date with destiny in Russia. I'm still feeling the effects of my head injury, but there's no way it's going to stop me being a part of this World Cup. I can't wait. Only six days until the first match kicks off.

Our training base is located in Istra, about 30 miles outside Moscow. It's in a magnificent setting, but we're surprised to find that the hotel is in the middle of nowhere, surrounded by forest. The French Football Federation (FFF) has made sure the hotel and grounds are available for our exclusive use, both for security reasons and so that we can concentrate and work in optimum conditions. Even the mosquitoes that plague the area seem unable to make it through the heavy gate into the estate. A member of staff assigns us our bedrooms. Everyone has their own room, each one decorated with a specially commissioned portrait of the player who occupies it. I smile when I see the mural that represents me.

A little later, we take a tour of the estate and hope our stay here is a long one. There is a cinema, swimming pool, two tennis courts, a pétanque court and even a small lake. We cover six miles just getting to the training ground. The pitch is immaculate. It all looks amazing. Despite the rain, morale is high. We do our first training session behind closed doors. The next day, the manager will allow one session to be open to the public – just a little gesture of appreciation for the French fans who have made the trip to Russia to support us.

Friday, 15 June. One day to go before France–Australia. In the afternoon we head to training, the last session before our first World Cup game. We still don't know which 11 players will be starting it. The coach usually tells us the day before, so that we can prepare ourselves mentally. On rare occasions it's announced two or three hours before the match, just before the team talk. Maybe the opposite applies here: it's to stop us from having too much time to think.

Didier Deschamps doesn't give us the news personally. We learn who has been selected through who gets to wear a bib. Let me explain: in the 11-a-side match we play in training, only those players who will be in the starting line-up wear bibs. The manager hands these players their bib just before we start our warm-up. We call this the 'legend of the bibs'. This afternoon, my world falls apart: there's no bib for me. I'm not going to be starting against Australia. Deschamps has made a tactical decision to play Antoine Griezmann, Kylian Mbappé and Ousmane Dembélé in the forward line. I try my best to save face and don't let my feelings show. All the same, I'm pretty fed up.

In this last training match with the team, I receive the ball and run towards goal. N'Golo Kanté comes after me. He's so close behind me that I can feel his breath on the back of my neck. It's such a comical moment that it takes my mind off everything. The pitch is a bit dry. I speed up. Lucas Hernandez appears in front of me, N'Golo catches me and somehow my feet get tangled in each other, I stumble and down I go. My head collides with my team-mate's knee on the exact same spot I was injured before. I stay on the ground. It hurts like hell. I take off my bandage and the blood starts pouring. Two stitches have just come out.

This is unreal. I'm not starting the match and if that wasn't bad enough, I'm thinking this injury might take me out of the World Cup altogether. I leave the pitch and hurry to see the medic who's waiting for me in the dressing room. On the way there, I lose it and vent my rage by giving a billboard a massive kick. If the media had been around, as they sometimes are, I'd never have let myself express my anger like that. There are no journalists anywhere to be seen. Impulsive, yes. Out of control, never.

I'm gutted. The manager, who misses nothing, notices how distressed I am. He waits until after dinner that evening to speak to me face to face about his decision.

I try and predict how he's going to explain it. Since I'm still wearing my bandage and I have fresh stitches in my head wound, I believe for a split second that he's decided to leave me on the bench to protect me, and ask him, 'Is it because of my injury? You want to spare me, is that it?'

'No. You're not going to play because I've made a tactical decision.'

The decision is final. He ends our conversation by saying, 'I'm asking you not to show your disappointment before the match.'

I'm really taken aback. Questions are racing through my mind. Why is the manager not starting me? Why did he change the game plan for this first match? I don't necessarily share his point of view, but it's not the first time that I've found myself dealing with this kind of situation. I give up. It's hard and it hurts a lot, but I accept it.

All I can do is get on with things and maintain a positive mindset for my team. Put the squad before myself. The mind plays a crucial role when you're trying to pick yourself up from a setback. I'm going to draw strength from deep within me to overcome my disappointment. And then there is my faith. I pray and ask Jesus to help me turn the situation to my advantage. I have to perform to the best of my ability.

After dinner I call Jen, my wife, who's there for me in good times and bad. She's the only person who can calm me down. She's detached enough from the situation and can find the right words, 'Be patient, keep the faith and stay focused. Your time will come and you have to be ready for it.' My brother Romain, my biggest fan, also lends me his support.

The night feels like it's never going to end. I'm restless and I can't get to sleep. My situation is emotionally hard to deal with. There are intrusive thoughts swirling round my head that I can't seem to shake off. But I have to stay focused on one goal: victory for the French team, with or without me.

I deserve my place

It's time for the first match. Sitting on the bench, I swallow my pride and get behind my team-mates. France are struggling to score. The threesome up front are not showing much sign of igniting. I've been warming up since the start of the second half and in the 70th minute the manager sends me on. This is my chance. I have to bring something to the team and my performance has to make a difference. Deschamps often tells us that substitutes play an important role. I want to be that player who changes the course of the match. Now it's time to prove that I deserve my place on the team. The adrenaline rises. I put my emotions aside and step out on to the pitch.

The teams are tied 1-1. We're getting mauled by the Australians, so we have to respond and score a second goal. Ten minutes from time, entering the penalty area, Paul Pogba plays a one-two with me and shoots. His shot is deflected by the opposing defender Aziz Behich, hits the crossbar, then bounces over the Australian goal line by a couple of inches; 2-1! But FIFA later rules it to be an own goal by Behich. If the governing body hadn't robbed Paul of that goal, it would have been my assist. But that doesn't matter. Thanks to us, France have just won their first group match. Mission accomplished. I've got my starting slot back. From that day on, I don't take my bib off.

'We can't win with Giroud on the team'

I've come to terms with the media. It's part of my job to shield myself from the anti-Giroud flak I regularly get bombarded with. I hardly ever use social media and I don't read the papers very often either, but that doesn't stop certain news reports reaching me. This time the comments are positive. I'm not under any illusions: if I'd messed up my opening World Cup game, the journalists wouldn't have thought twice before starting to question my credentials again. But after that first match, I read, 'It would be good to see players other than Giroud on form, but when he isn't on the team, it's clear something's missing.' And, 'The team miss Olivier when he's not playing.'

I'm not the only striker on this team, of course. No one is irreplaceable. But these words make me feel good all the same.

After my performance against Australia, the manager starts me against Peru. This is another match that we have to win if we're going to get into the knockout stage without a struggle. It's more than a match. It's a duel that's played out in front of a hostile crowd. Peru, who haven't qualified for the World Cup since 1982, have managed to get 35,000 of their supporters into the 40,000 seats in the stadium. While their national anthem plays, the noise of the crowd creates such a white-hot atmosphere that I get a shiver down my spine. It feels like we're actually in South America. The air is tense. During the warm-up, listening to the crowd booing, I say to Paul Pogba, 'We didn't become footballers to end up playing a match like this, did we?'

'We need to take this hostility and use it to our advantage,' he replies.

He's right. Adversity gets us riled up. It turbocharges us. I start the match with the mindset of a warrior and get involved in the action every time; lay-off passes, flicking headers, shadowing the Peruvian defender to create space for my team-mates. I badly want to score. In the 34th minute, Paul finds me with a pass. I shoot, but it's blocked. Kylian, on the prowl in front of the goal, nabs the ball and taps it into the net. He didn't have to touch it – the ball was headed straight for the goal. I didn't want to pass – it was a shot on goal I was after. I should have scored but Kylian was there on the line and, like any self-respecting striker would, he stepped in and took the shot. Later, I'm asked if I'm mad at him for 'stealing' that goal from me. Absolutely not, is my answer. In his place, I'd have done exactly the same. The striker is the most selfish player on a team, and he has to be. In the penalty area he thinks of himself – and, by extension, the team. Kylian has done what is expected of him. We talk about it after the match, and the incident (which is not even an incident) is resolved right away.

This is not me just being nice. I understand what he did and how happy he was to score his first World Cup goal. The way I responded is also in keeping with the kind of person I am deep down: altruistic and generous, on and off the pitch. This may sound a little boastful, but it's just the way I was brought up. There are still matches left to play, there will be plenty more opportunities to score.

A gang of mates

Away from the tournament and off the pitch, the French team has become a tight-knit bunch over the years, thanks to Didier Deschamps. Despite the age gap between the youngest (19 years old) and the oldest (33), and the differences in our tastes and lifestyles, we respect each other. We're a gang of mates.

During the day, we're focused and we take our work seriously, then in the evenings we relax. After dinner, some of us sit putting the world to rights, and others listen to music in their room or play cards. The atmosphere is calm and relaxed. Well, with the exception of a few evenings.

After the match against Peru, we need to decompress, to forget about football for a few hours. We've already qualified for the knockout stage so the game against Denmark is academic. We want to celebrate this first achievement and get away from our base camp. A summit is held: how can we persuade the manager to give us a bit of freedom? Adil Rami comes to our rescue and speaks up, 'I'm going to ask him. Guys, we've nothing to lose. If he says no, well too bad, at least we've tried.'

Deschamps is sitting a few metres away. He's talking to his staff and looks relaxed. This seems as good a time as any. We go up to him timidly, like kids facing their teacher. The manager smiles knowingly when he sees us.

'If Rami's here, something's going on. It's not a good sign,' he laughs, and then continues, 'Go on, then, what is it?'

'We need to take a breather and clear our heads a bit. We'd like to leave the camp and go and have dinner somewhere.'

Without any hesitation, the manager agrees to our request. We're amazed that we didn't need to argue our case and yet at the same time, we're not that surprised we got our own way. Deschamps is fair and humane, and one of his main qualities is empathy. He has the ability to put himself in our shoes. This evening, he understands that for the good of the squad he needs to relax the pressure and give us a bit of freedom. The next match isn't for another five days.

Several Mercedes people-carriers belonging to the FFF are chartered for the occasion. Destination Moscow, over an hour's drive away. We're surrounded by members of our security staff who watch over us discreetly but effectively. The restaurant where we have dinner has not been closed to the public, but orders are given that we are not to be disturbed. The other diners are discreet and respectful, with the exception of three young people who ask us for selfies, which we readily agree to. We're over the moon to get a taste of real life. We allow ourselves a few drinks, we have a laugh, we talk about everything and nothing – but hardly at all about football – then we go back to Istra, revived and refreshed, and ready to continue the fight.

Our second jaunt to the outside world doesn't go quite the same way as the first. It takes place a few hours after our stunning victory against Argentina. We've made it through to the quarter-finals and we're as high as kites, so much so that a little overindulgence is the only thing that might calm us down.

The evening begins quietly enough. We're on a private barge. It's in a magnificent setting, the food is delicious and the wines have been carefully chosen. We're drinking a bit more than last time. As the evening goes on, the atmosphere becomes more celebratory and reaches a peak on our way back to base camp.

When we get back to the hotel, the group splits up and I find myself with Hugo Lloris and Lucas Hernandez, both of them pretty merry. It's pitch black outside. Lucas is singing. He wanders closer to the pool and all of a sudden jumps right in, fully clothed. Helped along by the booze, he narrowly avoids swallowing half the pool and only just manages to grab hold of the side. The three of us are cracking up. It's a night I'll certainly not forget for a long time and one of my fondest memories of that World Cup.

As though things weren't already hysterically funny, that same evening Adil Rami earns notoriety through his brilliant handling of a fire extinguisher. I'm not going to dwell on this episode, which has been recounted more than enough times in minute detail. Suffice to say it was a unique and quite unforgettable experience.

On top of the world

Life goes on in Istra. We get back to work in earnest and gradually find our focus again for our quarter-final against Uruguay, which we win 2-0. I'm happy with my performance, especially in the head-to-head battles against some of the best defenders at this World Cup. The tournament continues. We're winning matches, but I've yet to find the back of the net. I make no secret of the fact that for a striker, this is hard to take. I've got enough strength of character, however, that I don't lose confidence in myself or in my abilities. Oddly enough, the media stays off my back and actually praises what I bring to the team. There is still criticism from some quarters, but I just keep chugging along.

And I do it pretty well, actually. I don't score, but I supply assists and I'm effective on the pitch – except, that is, in the semi-final against Belgium. I take unrealistic shots and I don't react quickly enough during one passage of play in particular. I don't anticipate the ball coming, so when it reaches me I'm not ready. I miss my shot. I could have and should have scored. I talk about it a bit later with Guy Stéphan, the assistant manager, 'I'm saving the goal for the final.'

The goal never comes.

We beat Belgium 1-0. The manager lets us have dinner with our friends and families. Jennifer, my dad and my father-in-law join me, as do Didier, Momo, Baptiste and Mat – 'my bros', as I call them. They wouldn't have missed an opportunity to see me play for anything in the world. We've been friends for many years. Outside my family, the four of them are my rocks and I can always count on them for support. We are joined together like the five fingers of a hand. In fact, I sometimes dedicate goals to them by holding up my five fingers. I did this after my goal against Switzerland in the 2014 World Cup in Brazil.

Sunday, 15 July. The final. Victory. I'll never forget what we experienced that night. Apart from the exhilaration that comes from actually winning the title, it's having my daughter Jade by my side that gets me most emotional. After the excitement has subsided, I go and get her from the stands and lead her on to the pitch. She's only five, but I can sense that she gets how important this moment is. I lift her up and we have a photo taken together with the trophy in our arms. Jen arrives a few minutes later. We embrace and she whispers in my ear that she's proud of me.

I became a footballer out of passion and every day I'm thankful I can make a living from it. I play to win, to build a successful career and to create a secure future, but I also play for those I love. They're starry-eyed tonight, and it's down to me. They deserve this so much. They support me, whatever I do, whatever decisions I make, whatever happens to me. They suffer the blows directed at me just as much as I do; they're nervous when I play, they rejoice when I score. This World Cup belongs to them as much as it belongs to me. We won it together and we will celebrate it together.

After a party in the dressing room, an even bigger party awaits us in Istra. The journey from the stadium back to our base camp gives us an opportunity to finally be together, just us. We are on a total high. It's getting noisier and noisier down at the front of the bus where the staff sit. Even the manager, normally so composed, really lets himself go, making the driver jump as he hammers out a rhythm on the bus windows to acknowledge the supporters. Presnel Kimpembe, the squad's part-time DJ, takes his mission very seriously and plays rap hits, with Thomas Lemar, Kylian Mbappé, Paul Pogba and Blaise Matuidi all rapping along with the music. Benjamin Mendy, shirtless, stands in the aisle of the bus, swaying his hips and singing at the top of his lungs. The champagne flows freely. We are ecstatic.

We get to the hotel around 1am, where we're greeted for the final time by the staff who, as usual, have formed a guard of honour. This ritual was established right at the start of the tournament. Every time we returned from a match, the hotel staff did this to celebrate our victory.

We push through the crowd, holding the trophy aloft, passing it from player to player. Our families and loved ones, just as hyper as us, are already waiting for us in the hotel restaurant. The FFF has made sure they've been well looked after. Jennifer and Jade are there. I hadn't managed to see my parents at the stadium, but I find them now.

'I'm proud of you, son. Well done!' my father says, with tears in his eyes. I've never seen him so emotional. My mother too is proud of her 'little chick' – the nickname she's had for me since the day I was born. I'll always be their 'little Olivier'. Tonight, little Olivier is a world champion and he is going to celebrate his title as he should.

As footballers, our diet largely consists of pasta and white meat. We stuck to this throughout the tournament, but now it makes way for barbecue and all kinds of sweet treats. We're standing on the tables, draining our champagne glasses in time with the songs we're improvising. We sing our own version of Joe Dassin's hit 'Les Champs-Élysées', changing the lyrics in honour of our midfielder N'Golo Kanté. Benjamin Pavard also gets his moment of musical glory with a rendition of a song that fans came up with after his stunning goal against Argentina. Then it's Paul Pogba's turn to set the dance floor on fire with his brothers, Mathias and Florentin. Watched with amusement by DJ Snake, who came over for the occasion, the three siblings perform a series of dance routines, shaking their hips wildly to the music.

The party goes on until 3am. As the room gradually empties, the sun is already rising in this corner of Russia. Our families, tiredness now showing on their faces, go up to bed. We can't join them yet. We still haven't come back down to earth from the euphoria that started as soon as the referee blew the final whistle. For us, the party has only just begun.

A few of us make our way towards a mud-filled lake. Florence Hardouin, the FFF's general manager, our head waiter Raphaël, Bach, our kit man, and other FFF employees are there too. We hesitate for a moment before, one by one, we get into the thick brown water. Some of us are in our underwear. Others, like Florence, go in fully dressed. Our shouting and singing ring out louder than ever. We're immune to the cold and fatigue.

In the craziness of the moment, Lucas Hernandez comes to find Raphaël and shaves his head in front of everyone. At around 5, we round off the night with a game of pétanque near our training centre.

Everything has to come to an end. A few hours later, this incredible adventure draws to a close. After more than two months together, the time has come to go our separate ways. We're so tired that we keep our goodbyes short. Our families by our sides, each of us leaves for a well-deserved holiday.

Back down to earth

Jen, the kids and I are off to the south of France. A completely different kind of celebration awaits us: the christening of Aaron, just six months old. All our family and friends who didn't have the chance to travel to Russia join us in Èze, at the Hotel Cap-Estel, a timelessly idyllic spot. Another opportunity to pursue the dream. After the baptism, it's time for me to honour a bet I made a few weeks earlier with journalists from TF1. One of them had asked me what I'd be prepared to do if I won the World Cup. As I get a lot of stick from my team-mates about my hair, I replied without thinking, 'I'd shave my head for a laugh.'

True to my word, on the evening after my son's christening, I end up with my head like a billiard ball. Needless to say, my new look did nothing to shut my friends up and they carried right on taking the mickey.

Next, we spend a few days in Monaco, then Jen and I leave our three children in Grenoble with their grandparents and jet off for a romantic trip to Ibiza.

Now the pressure's easing, I feel tired. I need to get away from it all – to escape from all the rejoicing, cut myself off from the outside world for a while and enjoy some peace and quiet with my wife, just the two of us. The destination we've chosen isn't the most relaxing one, but we do what we can to avoid the crowds. We visit amazing places, we take a boat trip, we walk along the beach and we talk a lot. Gradually, I come back down to earth. It isn't easy. How do you reach these heights and then start all over again without being mentally affected by it all? This is what top-level athletes have to go through.

At times like these, I appreciate just how important my close friends and family are, especially my wife and kids. They help me get through this bad patch. When I look at Jade, Evan and Aaron, I tell myself that I'm not allowed to flag. And so I don't flag. They give me the strength and the will to battle on, and when I'm with them I don't have enough time to indulge my moods. Having three young children keeps you busy. They have this amazing ability to put things into perspective for me. I stop focusing on my own needs and they become my priority. They come before football, before myself, before everything.

My wife goes through – endures, you might say – these difficult times with a mixture of strength, intelligence and compassion. I'm not doing so great in the weeks following our World Cup victory. Other players have spoken about going through 'a tough time' or 'a mild depression'. I can confirm that. By the time I go back to Chelsea, things have reached quite a critical point. I'm lethargic. I have no energy at all. It's like a kind of natural decompression that comes in the form of mental fatigue, but along with that there's a weird sensation that I haven't made the most of this unique moment in my life, that I haven't celebrated it enough. I'm getting the suspicion that the feeling of winning the World Cup will just fade away with time and will slip from my grasp.

My friend Antonio Rüdiger, who plays for Chelsea, keeps calling me 'Olivier, 2018 World Cup winner!' As if to say, 'No one can ever take that title away from you.' Which is true. Even today, people I meet on the street thank me for what we did. I'm a world champion for life, but I'm going to need a hell of a lot of strength of character to re-motivate myself, lace up my football boots and get out there for another season.

Getting a star on your national jersey is without a doubt the highest point of a career in football. It's hard to go bigger, better or further than a World Cup victory for your country. I'm not downplaying the other titles. The Champions League is prestigious, but when it comes to playing for a city versus playing for your country, for 67 million French people there is no comparison. I am a patriot. I love my country, I'm proud to represent it and to have worn our national colours at the highest level. But there's no way I'm going to stop there.

I will bounce back.

During a conversation in the Chelsea dressing room, my team-mates ask me why I'm not calling time on my international career. 'You're a world champion, you should quit while you're ahead. It'll be very hard to go one better than that. Or even to consolidate it by winning the Euros.'

I hear their arguments, but the thought of leaving the squad has never crossed my mind. I'm too attached to the French team, I'm hungry for more victories. I don't want to quit too soon and then regret it. I still have goals to score and matches to win. Football is about starting all over again, time and time again.

Winning a World Cup doesn't make me a different person. I'm delighted I have done that, but I don't get too carried away. I never will. I remember everything I've gone through to get to this point.

During tough times, I've always managed to stay positive while I wait for better days to arrive. I remain true to my motto: work, respect and humility. I have my parents to thank for this mindset. They've never changed either, and nor has the way they see me. I'm surrounded by family, in-laws and friends who look after my wellbeing no matter what. Always calm and collected, never going overboard. I can't take any credit for this. I'm just out of the same mould, that's all.

If there is a before and after, it comes from the outside world. The manager warned us about this, right after our victory when we were all together in the dressing room. 'There is nothing more beautiful, nothing greater than lifting the World Cup. From today, your lives are going to change. You'll never be the same again. You know why?' He held up the cup and yelled, 'World champions!'

He was right. Our popularity is off the scale. We're known and recognised around the world. Publicists and PR people are getting in touch, all kinds of requests are piling up. We are awarded the Legion of Honour, France's highest distinction, and welcomed into a very select circle of people who have contributed to the nation's global renown. Mind you, it's worth mentioning that there is an important distinction to be made between athletes like us who inspire others, and people who actually fight for our country. We have to keep things in perspective.

This new-found fame, it makes life good, I don't deny it. It gives me a confidence boost. But deep down, I don't change. I'm still my parents' son, Jen's husband and my kids' dad. I might be a world champion, but I'll never forget where I come from.

2

Childhood

HANGING ON for dear life is the story of my existence, and it has been that way right from the start.

This story begins very early. In my mother's womb. I am an accident. After three children, my parents think the family is complete. For the first few weeks I grow, nestled inside my mother, who is unaware of my tiny presence.

I learn the story of my conception when I'm a teenager. Mum and I are home alone when she decides to broach the subject with me. This secret has been eating away at her for many years. She has prayed a lot, trying to find the courage to share this truth with me.

I can't remember all the details of that day, only that we're in the kitchen. My mother looks at me steadily, but her eyes betray her fear of how I'm going to react. She speaks so sincerely, so unceremoniously, in fact, that her words are almost violent. A cry from the heart. 'You weren't wanted,' she says. She adds immediately, 'But you know, as soon as you arrived, we were delighted to welcome you.' The clarification is unnecessary. I've never doubted for a second my parents' love for me.

Reassured by how calmly I'm taking all this, she tells me how she felt during her nine months of pregnancy, 'I had a terrible inner struggle. A constant spiritual battle. The pain came from deep within me, because I didn't want a fourth child. Your dad and I thought the family was big enough with three of you. We had never planned for it to be any other way.'

I know that for religious reasons, my mother would never have considered a termination. That solution was out of the question from the very beginning. And so she found herself trapped.

This conversation could have upset me, destroyed me even, but it didn't at all. I've had so much love from my family that when the revelation finally came, it had no impact on me. It's nothing more than a small detail, a non-event. Nonetheless, it's a non-event that started everything off. My own legend, so to speak, and where I think my will to survive originates.

We stay in the kitchen for a while. The tension eases and we speak more freely. We both feel quite emotional. Mum is relieved. As she often says, it's best to get everything out in the open. She has shed the burden that has been weighing her down for a long time. It has been a cathartic conversation for both of us.

I've often thought back on all this, realising that even in the womb I was in a battle for survival. In fact, what I've become has stemmed in part from this battle I was fighting before I was even born, one that set me up for life. It motivated me, it shaped my character and it gave me the strength to face challenges head on. Were it not for this 'accident' I might not be where I am today.

The cherry on the cake

I make my first appearance on 30 September 1986, at the Sainte-Marie hospital in Chambéry. The doubts and anxiety that have plagued my mother for the last nine months give way to immense joy. My brother Bertrand is ten and a half, Romain is nine and Bérengère five and a half. I am the star attraction, the blue-eyed boy, the unwelcome stranger who has turned out to be the cherry on the cake. Everyone is delighted with their unexpected back-to-school present, even my sister, whose status as baby of the family I've just stolen. There's a photo I remember that shows Bertrand, Romain, Bérengère and their friends leaning over my Moses basket looking down at me adoringly.

A few days after my birth, we go home to our house in Froges. This is where I grow up – a small town in the east of France, a few miles from Grenoble. At the time it had a population of 4,000. I imagine there are twice as many people living there now. We live in a two-storey house. My parents have had a swimming pool built in the garden. A little further away, there is a swing and some apple trees, which we will eventually have to cut down as they're diseased. There are also raspberries, a cherry tree and a couple of fir trees, including a very small silver fir that my grandfather planted the year I was born. I regularly measure my height against my twin tree. At the back of the garden stands a small shed for storing wood. We love spending winter evenings in front of the fire.

My whole family is from this region of France. My maternal grandparents live in a nice house 100 metres away. My grandpa is a cheesemaker. He goes to milk the cows in the mountains, then makes the cheese. His job really stirs my imagination. I'm ten when I start to take an interest in what he does. By this time, he has retired. 'Grandpa,' I say to him, 'I'm jealous because you took my brothers to milk the cows and you didn't take me!' My grandma sells the cheese in the local cheese shop which they own. It's a real success story.

I am very close to my grandparents. Almost every day when I get out of school, I stop by their house to have a snack and watch TV, before heading home to do my homework. Sometimes I play rummy with my grandma. She lets me win, until the day comes when I can play better than her. Her name is Antonia and, of my four grandparents, she's the only one I have left. She still lives in the same house.

My childhood can be summed up in a single phrase: one big happy family. My parents hardly ever argue. They're still together and are very close. They are my role models and I try to follow the example they've set. Starting a family, loving and feeling loved in return, and protecting those we hold dear: that's what keeps us going, what makes us able to move mountains, what keeps us standing when the going gets tough. My family are my rock, my roots and my wings.

The end of innocence

I sail through my early years without a care in the world. Until one day, this happy-go-lucky attitude is suddenly shattered by the loss of someone close. I'm 12 years old when Philippe, my brother Romain's best friend, is killed in a car accident. He was 20 and was like a member of our family. My parents used to hang out with his, and Philippe spent a lot of time at our house. He and Romain were inseparable. The gang of friends lost one of its key members that day.

I'm at home with Bertrand, Romain and some friends when Philippe's brother tells us the terrible news. I'm so stunned that I don't react at first. My parents come home right away. I see in their eyes the incomprehension and profound shock give way to a feeling of utter devastation. For the first time, I'm faced with the reality of death. I become aware that everything can change from one minute to the next. I am a child and this is all news to me.

I lie down on the sofa and burst into tears. I cry for a long, long time, flipping from sadness to anger and back again, 'It's not fair! It's so cruel! How can God let this happen?' It will take me a good while to get over this tragedy, the first one I've had to deal with in my short life. Even today, I'm still in touch with Philippe's parents and his brother, all of whom I'm very close to.

The magical thing about the passage of time is that pain and sorrow recede, although they're never completely erased. They end up forming a kind of calm horizon. I have never forgotten what happened, but life went on, bringing its share of simple pleasures, fun and laughter, and a sense of frivolity that comes from being young.

Keep on moving

I'm a cheerful and mischievous child, always surrounded by friends. I can't stand being on my own. I stick to my brothers like glue whenever I can, otherwise I call one of my friends to invite them over to play at mine or kick a football around. Something always has to be happening and I constantly have to be on the move. I'm bursting with energy, bordering on hyperactive. In the evening, exhausted by the day, I sometimes fall asleep at the table while I'm having dinner with my family.

I'm also very affectionate, probably because I receive so much love. My mother never misses an opportunity to give me a hug. It's nothing at all to do with guilt on her part: she's never felt any sort of guilt towards me. She just loves to cuddle me. Nothing has changed. Now I'm an adult, our relationship is still just as loving. Every time I see her, I want to hug her. I need to hug her.

We're very close. It's my mum who raises us. My dad is a senior manager in a food processing company and works long hours. He is there for us as much as he can be, but he has so little spare time. He leaves the house at four o'clock in the morning and doesn't come home until late at night. I make the most of him being around on Sunday mornings when I sneak into my parents' bed and he cuddles me while we wait for mum to bring the coffee.

My dad is a loving and charismatic man. When he speaks we listen to him. He doesn't have to tell us twice when he wants us to do something. But I must admit that it's Mum we're scared of.

She used to work as a secretary in her parents' business but after my second brother was born she gave up work to be a stay-at-home mum. She took our upbringing seriously to say the least. She has an iron will and a forceful personality. She's very sweet, very sociable. She doesn't always say much, but when she does speak her words carry a lot of weight. Since my dad is away so much, she has to be both mother and father to us. Then, she is strict, authoritarian and demanding. We don't ever risk acting smart with her; we're far too scared to. She refuses to compromise on anything when it comes to our upbringing.

Stepping out of line earns us a smack. Sometimes we even get hit with a strap. She tells us that 'hands are made for stroking, not for hitting'. I think she's afraid of hurting herself. My mother is far from the wicked witch of fairy tales, but with four lively, at times somewhat agitated children, she can't afford to relax.

My parents rarely get involved in our arguments or quarrels. We're lucky that we can express ourselves quite openly in our family. We can do as we please as long as we don't cross the line. There weren't many restrictions placed on us when we were children, but all the same our mother instilled values in us very early on. The difference between right and wrong, treat others as you'd like to be treated yourself. She moulded our characters according to the principles of moral rigour, hard work and selflessness. She insisted that we were respectful, polite and obedient.

I try to follow her example when it comes to bringing up my own children.

Values

Even from when we were young, my mother taught us the value of money. We never wanted for anything, but every penny counted, and there was never any question of relaxing that principle. She hated waste and never threw anything away. With a large family like ours, she had to be thrifty.

As a kid, I remember asking her to buy me the latest pair of cool trainers. She refused and explained why. I was really upset, but the lesson wasn't lost on me. What my mother taught us came in useful when I first started earning my own money.

I am fortunate to be able to provide my family with a very nice, very comfortable lifestyle. We had a lovely apartment in London, we have a nanny for the children, a personal chef and various other perks. In short, we have a good life.

I've been a professional footballer for many years, and everyone has a pretty good idea of the salaries and bonuses we earn. I could have spent like there was no tomorrow and blown it all. Yet while I don't deprive myself or my wife and children, I've always been careful. First of all out of principle, but also because this supply of money is not infinite and our careers as footballers are very short. It's quite literally game over by the time we're 40. I've given some thought to this less prosperous future and made sure we have a nest egg. Every penny counts, even when you have a lot of pennies.

I do all I can to pass these values on to my children. They are too little to realise what we have, but I try to explain to them how lucky they are and the fact that they are very privileged. From time to time, when I think I've spoiled them enough, I also refuse to buy them the presents they ask for. It doesn't matter how disappointed they are, I know one day, like me at that age, they will understand.

3

Religion

My reality

I am very religious. This is my reality. It can come as a surprise to people and might seem a little old-fashioned these days, especially in an athlete. But I'm comfortable with my faith and I talk about it publicly.

I'm not the only one in this industry to believe in God. There are practising Catholics, Muslims too, like my friend Paul Pogba, who converted to Islam a few years ago. We tease each other good-naturedly about it, but we respect each other's beliefs.

I discover religion around the age of four, when I go to church with my mum on Sunday mornings. The atmosphere there is very solemn, yet joyful at the same time. Music forms a large part of the service. I watch the worshippers sing and dance, their eyes closed. The air is heavy with emotion, so much so that sometimes a member of the congregation will actually pass out for a few seconds. There is no priest, but a pastor. No actual church, but a large hall. No candles, no organ, no statues of saints or the Virgin Mary, only a large cross.

I'm not at a Catholic mass, but an evangelical worship service. Evangelism is a branch of Protestantism. My family is originally Catholic. My maternal grandparents – especially my grandfather – go to church regularly and observe important holidays. My mother was brought up in this religion, but when she was 18 or so, she felt a deep inner void that prompted her to ask some existential questions. One day, chance – I'd rather call it fate – leads her to cross paths with a young couple who have just moved into the house opposite. On their mailbox is a poster. On it, a finger points to the sky, with the words, 'One way: Jesus'. At first, my mum thinks it must be some sort of cult.

A few days later, she is invited over for coffee with these neighbours and, curious to know more, asks them about this phrase she finds so intriguing. They explain that they're evangelical Christians. 'You acknowledge that you're a sinner. The Bible alone is the final authority and the basis of our religion. One way: Jesus.'

These few words are all it takes to convince her to follow this path. She abandons the Catholic faith to join the evangelical church, placing her life in the hands of God. It's self-evident, as it is for all people who seek God. A new birth. Finally, she has found the answers to most of the questions she has been asking.

According to the evangelical faith, you are not born a Christian, you become one through personal choice and individual commitment. We speak of individual and deliberate conversion to Jesus Christ, or being born again in reference to adult baptism. Unlike infant baptism in the Catholic religion, baptism can only be carried out when the person in question is of an age to publicly express their faith. This faith is based on an inner transformation lived by the believer, who places their trust in God and decides to apply the teachings of Christ to their life.

Unlike Catholics, for whom the clergy act as intermediaries with the divine, we evangelicals have a direct relationship with Jesus. We are committed to sharing the Gospel and are regularly accused of proselytising. Which is not true. Our mission is to spread the universality of the Gospel message, but with respect for everyone's freedom of choice. This is what evangelism is.

My media profile means that a large number of people listen to what I say. I use my fame to talk about Jesus and tell people more about him. I spread the Christian Gospel, but without ever forcing it down anyone's throat or spouting propaganda. Everyone is free to believe or not.

I also put my faith to good use for causes that are close to my heart. Persecuted Christians around the world are one such cause.

From a very young age, my brothers, sister and I have been steeped in this belief. My dad too, but he expresses his faith less openly than my mum. Bertrand and Romain were baptised Catholics at birth. My mother had left the Catholic Church a while before but she didn't want to upset the family harmony by refusing a traditional baptism. It was still too early for that.

Bérengère, on the other hand, was brought up as an evangelical Christian right from the start. One day, she was at church with my mum where she witnessed two adults being baptised. The preacher who was officiating suggested to the congregation that they could convert if they felt the urge or the need. My sister spontaneously stood up and, without even asking my mum what she thought, went up on to the stage. A few months later, she was baptised in a small church. She was 25.

As for me, it may sound strange but I'm baptised a Catholic at the age of 19. Although a committed evangelist, I agree to this baptism so that I can be godfather to Louis, my brother Romain's son, and also to be able to marry Jennifer in church a little further down the line. I take classes with a priest and go to meetings where we talk about religion and study Bible texts, and I attend religious study classes. I am what is called a catechumen, someone who wants to be baptised a Christian. I find this time very personally fulfilling and I become well informed about the life of Christ.

The day of my baptism comes. I'm wearing a white robe. During the ceremony, the priest makes the sign of the cross on my forehead. Deep down, I know I belong here, even though this is not my church. I feel the need to come before the Lord and say to Him, 'I am being baptised before you. I give you my life.'

A long road

My belief in Jesus has grown over the years. I use the word 'grown' because it correctly implies that I have a staunch faith now, but that getting to that point was a gradual process.

When I was very little, I read children's books on the subject. I learned songs and prayers. I went to religious classes and studied verses from the Bible, fascinated by the many characters who lived in those ancient times. Religion consolidates the core values my mother has passed on to us: respect, humility, kindness, sharing and love.

A little later on, my parents send me to a Christian youth camp for the holidays. These are summer camps run by pastors and activity leaders. I'm happy to go there as I meet up with my friends and we play different sports and do fun activities. During the day, we stop for an hour of quiet reflection. It's a time for prayer, during which we read the Bible and sing, sometimes around a campfire.

At that age, we're preoccupied by much less spiritual concerns, but all the same, I care a lot about the subject. I'm getting to know Jesus.

My mother is my guide on this path. She explains that God sacrificed His only son to save us from our sins. It's not easy for me, as a little boy, to interpret this or to understand it. However, there is one thing I'm certain of, and that's that Jesus exists, God exists and every time I pray I'm talking to Someone who is listening to me.

My faith did not come about overnight. When I was little, I would just follow what my mum did without really understanding any of it. When I'm around seven or eight, I start to take a little more interest in this religion. The church services impress me, especially when I see how impassioned the pastor is when he preaches. 'Wow,' I say to myself. 'It must be a powerful thing to be a Christian and feel like this.' I want to believe. And then I do believe.

When I'm 20, I get a psalm tattooed on my arm. I'm still living in Istres at this point. People from the south are big fans of tattoos. For my first tattoo I went for a tribal design on my calf, to make me look more like a footballer.

For my second I now have a very specific idea of what I want. A phrase that means something, and echoes my values and defines me as a man. It's no surprise that I choose Psalm XXIII, now inscribed on my forearm, 'The Lord is my Shepherd. I shall not want.' These few words are testament to the fact that God helps us keep going in good times and bad. He is a solid rock on which we can rest. He watches over us like a shepherd over his sheep.

The psalm continues, 'He makes me lie down in green pastures, He leads me beside still waters. He restores my soul. He leads me in paths of righteousness, for His name's sake.'

I have continued my spiritual journey through studying Bible texts and praying. I don't go to church often, for lack of time and because of my level of fame in England. But I think God is in all of us, so I pray often. Every evening, before I go to bed, I say a little prayer in my head. I thank God for His grace, I ask Him to protect my loved ones. To pray is also to repent, to ask for forgiveness.

I live with Him in my life every day. I turn to Him in times when I need help or guidance. I often pray when I'm on the pitch. It's enough just to say His name when I find myself in a difficult situation. I can already picture the mocking smiles of those who think I rely on God to score goals. Or, worse, that He makes them happen. No, I'm responsible for all my own actions. When I run on to the pitch, when I send the ball into the back of the net, it's definitely me and not Him. If I was waiting for God to help me score, I certainly wouldn't have made it this far. But football is about more than talent and legs. The mind plays a leading role too, and having a belief in a spiritual force helps me persevere, never give up and fight to the end.

When I score, I point my fingers towards heaven. I thank Him.

My lucky star

It would be pretentious of me to say that I've been 'chosen'. However, when I look back at the journey

I've taken, I have to face facts: I wasn't born with any exceptional talent, and yet I've played for big clubs, I've won cups, I'm a world champion. I was never meant to have this kind of career. I take the credit for all this success, but the love of Christ and my faith have enabled me to make the right choices and good decisions, and, most importantly, always believe in them.

I'm certain that I was born under a lucky star. I feel grateful and fortunate to have been spared so far from the great misfortunes that can happen in life.

I firmly believe that Jesus has a plan for each of us. 'A man's heart plans his course, but the Lord directs his steps' (*Proverbs* 16:9). This doesn't mean that we aren't the masters of our own destiny, but the encounters and the choices we make in our lives are not the result of chance.

As I see it, everything has a meaning.

What I'm saying might sound like superstition. This isn't the case. I do admit, though, that I have one compulsion I can't let go of. Any time I can use the number seven somewhere, I will do so. It's written in the Holy Scripture that the number seven is the perfect number. The seven days of Creation; seven pairs of clean animals of each species in Noah's ark; the righteous may fall seven times and rise again, forgiven; the seven patriarchs of Israel, and so on. So, for example, I always set my alarm clock for 7.07am or 7.37am. It's a way of including God in my daily life.

Throughout my spiritual quest, I've been lucky enough to meet people who have helped me get somewhere. Joël Thibault is a chaplain whose role is to support athletes in their faith. Some chaplains like this are attached to football clubs, others will come to major competitions from time to time to give their support to anyone who needs it.

One day, Couly, a friend of my mum's, told me about a pastor who works with English clubs. When he heard I was a believer, he wanted to get to know me.

We meet at Clairefontaine in March 2017, more than a year before the World Cup. I'm staying at the château, the castle used as a residence by the national squad, and he's there with a Christian football team lucky enough to have been invited to the training centre. We talk at length, then we decide to keep in touch.

He occasionally sends me religious texts to read, but my desire to learn is so great that he puts me in touch with someone I would call a spiritual coach, the Rev. Jean-Luc Sergent. Jean-Luc officiates at St Barnabas Church in Kensington, London and organises a weekly service in French for expats.

We've met regularly for several years now. We read passages from the Bible together, we talk about the Gospels. He answers my questions and enlightens me on the word of God. I even asked him to put together a sort of 'family tree' for Jesus, so that I could make sense of things more easily.

Nothing is ever enough to satisfy my longing to know more about the life of Christ and those around Him. The more I study, the more I admire His journey and the love He had for His neighbour. I draw lessons from my studies to help me become a better person. I learn forgiveness, because Jesus is a model of compassion.

I learn humility by trying my best to acknowledge my mistakes. I am human, a simple sinner who could go astray at any time. The main thing is to repent as sincerely as possible and not do it again.

Jesus's character inspires me to try to behave well in my daily life. He is for me a kind of benchmark, a role model. He gives me great inner strength. Thanks to Him, I never feel alone.

These are values I try to pass on to my children too. They are still too young to understand, but I give them books so that they can start learning about Jesus.

Every now and then my mum brings up the subject with my daughter Jade. One day, she said to her, 'You know, everything you see around you was created by God. Like a sunset, for example.' Since then, every time Jade sees the sun going down, she'll say, 'Look, Daddy, Jesus is in the sky! It's beautiful!'

I'll never force my kids to believe. I'm just trying to set them on the right path, and then they will form their own experiences and decide for themselves.

As for me, I'm continuing on my own journey, with all its ups and downs. I can't always find answers to the questions I ask myself – why is there so much misfortune, so much horror and disaster in the world? At other times, I rebel, like the day I mentioned when my brother's best friend died at the age of 20. But at no time do I ever question the existence of God.

I am a Christian, a believer. I have put my life in the hands of God, and if I ever get the chance, I would like to be baptised where Jesus was baptised: in the waters of the Jordan.

4

The Baby of the Family

Goldilocks

To listen to my brothers and sister, you'd think I'd
enjoyed special treatment because of my status as the
baby of the family. My parents were supposedly more
relaxed about everything by the time I came along.
No doubt this is why Bérengère gives me a really
hard time.

I'm nine, she's 14, and just hitting puberty.
Physically, she looks like butter wouldn't melt in her
mouth. She's blonde with big blue eyes. We call her
Goldilocks because of her curly hair – hair that she's

determined to straighten. But this angelic face masks a strong character. Very outspoken, she doesn't mince her words if something isn't to her liking.

Does she want to model herself on my mum? I don't know. Still, she never gives me an easy time of it. She can't stand me getting under her feet when she has her friends over. I'm desperate for her affection, but she just wants to be left alone. She often pushes me away, until one day one of her friends says, 'You're so tough on your brother, let him stay with us. He isn't bothering us.'

When she's 15, she meets Cédric, now her husband and the father of her children. She leaves home to make her own life. This separation doesn't affect our relationship in the slightest. We remain close.

My sister is a very private person. She follows my career from afar and has never interfered in my life. But she is there for me, just as I will always be there for her.

String, Romain and Two Socks

And then there are my older brothers, Bertrand – who I call 'String' because he's tall and thin – and Romain. Despite the ten years between Bertrand and me, I've never seen him as any kind of father figure. But when I was a kid, I was scared of him. Bertrand is the boss, the big brother. He's serious, organised, sensible and very charismatic. He's an imposing character. I know that you need to toe the line with him or you'll get your butt kicked. If I ever do anything remotely stupid, I live to regret it.

When it comes to doing stupid things, I'm not the only one. Back then, Bertrand used to read *Entrevue*, a magazine that featured celebrity interviews, although it also had an eye-catching cover that promised what delights lay in store if you were to flick through its pages. Photos of half-naked young women, accompanied by a couple of captions. I'm 13 or 14, just at the age when I'm beginning to feel the first stirrings of emotion, when I stumble upon these magazines lying around his room. My eye is irresistibly drawn to the photos.

While Bertrand is away, I sneak off with the forbidden magazines, make myself comfortable in my room and discreetly begin my sex education. Bertrand notices what I'm up to and says, 'I know what you're doing. Either you put those magazines back where you found them afterwards or you don't take them any more.' I'm relieved at his reaction, which simply means he did exactly the same when he was my age.

With Romain, the relationship is different. He is my hero, my role model, because he has my dream job. He is a footballer. I'm proud of him. He is the star of the village. Of the whole region, even. Other youngsters I meet or people who know him always ask after him and wish him good luck before a match. Romain has embarked on a brilliant career and has a great future ahead of him, it seems. Life, however, will decide otherwise, as I'll talk about in detail later.

I share his room. He sleeps in a bed; I'm on a mattress on the floor. Whenever he goes away for a few days to play for his club, I take his place in the bed and I try on his football kit. For his 17th birthday, he gets a bracelet engraved with his name. I'm eight years old and I'm thinking, 'When I grow up I'm going to wear a chain bracelet with my big brother's name on it too.' We are insanely close.

We look very alike, and our characters are similar too. He has nicknamed me 'Two Socks', after the wolf in the movie *Dances with Wolves*, because of my small eyes.

At 15, he joins the Auxerre youth academy. I spend my next few years growing up far away from him, but in my head he remains a kind of reference point, a fundamental part of my life. Whenever he comes home, we just pick up where we left off. I follow him everywhere he goes, I take naps with him. I get under his feet, just like I get under everyone's feet. I listen in to conversations, I push my way into games of football or whatever else people are trying to play, being the baby of the family I am.

'Say hello to Alf'

My brothers have their own special way of getting their own back on me for being in their way too much. This involves frequent references to Alf, the character from the TV series. Alf is a huge alien with a pig's nose. This creature makes my blood run cold. He haunts my childhood with his strange voice and his weird hands. The day my brothers realise just how scared I am of Alf, they use this to terrorise me. They wait for the perfect moment, just before bedtime when we're having dinner, and whisper in my ear, 'Oli, you'll need to say hello to Alf. He might be coming to see you tonight. He'll come in through the attic.' They fall about laughing while I sit frozen to my chair, struck dumb with terror.

Even today, I can't stand the sight of Alf. I don't trust that alien one bit.

Apart from these minor acts of cruelty, my brothers are kind to me. In Romain's bedroom there is a wardrobe with a hidden door inside that leads to the attic. I love this place, it's full of old treasures and toys that used to belong to Bertrand and Romain. Among other things, there's Playmobil, which I play with for hours on end. I invite my friends to play, then my brothers join in, helping us assemble the difficult parts. I also love board games and of course video games. I'm pretty good at *Mario Kart* and *Zelda*.

A little later, I'm allowed to join in the Sunday evening ritual. Romain and Geraldine – his wife at the time – have their close friends over. On the agenda: pizzas and boisterous games of Monopoly. I've been waiting for this moment all week. The grown-ups don't budge at all when I try and negotiate with them. In fact, I even suspect that they're taking advantage of my young age to rip me off. I don't let them walk all over me when I figure out what they're up to. It's fair enough, after all. I'm one of the gang.

5

Adolescence

The beautiful game

A photo. A very small child, a baby's bottle in his hand and a ball at his feet.

My passion for football takes holds of me when I'm still in nappies. A bit later, with my legs only just strong enough to support me, I start kicking a ball against a concrete wall originally designed for hitting tennis balls, 100 metres from our house. Unless someone summons me, I forget to go home.

I play when I get home from school, during every break – basically, whenever I can. I practise shots at goal and my shot power is already, let's say, respectable. To the point that I accidentally put a class-mate in hospital.

It's break time and a game of football gets going, just as it does during every break time. Leather balls are banned. We play with a foam ball instead, so that no one gets hurt if someone kicks it a bit too hard.

I'm in the six-yard box, standing with my back to the goal. The ball comes straight at me. I trap it and, without looking, I shoot on the turn, putting all my weight behind it. A boy who isn't even part of the game runs past. Wrong place, wrong time; he takes the ball on the arm. He freezes on the spot, falls to the ground, and starts screaming. A double fracture.

The little mountain apartment

I also love skiing. I live in an area surrounded by mountains and I hit the slopes for the first time when I'm just five years old. Alpine skiing, cross-country skiing, snowshoeing; I love anything you can do in the snow. Every school holiday, I go to Val-d'Isère with my cousin Matthieu to stay with our paternal grandparents, Henri and Yvonne, who have a modest apartment there. It has one bedroom and two bunk beds, a small bathroom and a small dining room. It might not be the lap of luxury but we have a great time. The apartment is right at the foot of the gondolas and the funicular, so our grandparents don't need to come with us. Skis on our shoulders, we set off on our own in the morning, returning home exhausted late in the afternoon. I'm enrolled in a ski school and I take part in competitions. A few years later, I reach 'Silver Arrow' level.

During the summers there, I do horse riding, archery, rock climbing and trampolining. Wonderful memories. My grandparents take good care of us and in this little apartment they create a warm atmosphere, a cosy cocoon where we like to take refuge after a good day on the slopes.

I miss the mountains. I had to leave all that behind when I started playing club football. Our contracts state that skiing is prohibited, as it's considered too high-risk a sport. When I lived in France with my wife, I allowed myself a few discreet getaways to the mountains. Having played in England and now that I'm in Italy, my schedule means this is no longer possible. I take comfort in the thought that I'll strap my skis back on once my career is over.

Remembering these past times gives me a deep sense of nostalgia. My grandparents passed away a few years ago. The idea of never returning to this place I loved so much was too hard to bear. I wanted to have something more tangible than my memories to hold on to. When I heard that my aunt was about to sell the apartment, I bought out her share and my dad's. It gives me pleasure to be able to let my family enjoy it now. It also means I've been able to keep a part of my grandparents with me.

Family holidays

These holidays are precious. I had very few opportunities to go away anywhere as a child. My mum never had the pleasure of travelling with her parents as they worked such long hours. Leisure activities were not a priority for them. She no doubt just kept the family tradition going.

I still have fond memories of a family holiday on the Costa Brava, in Spain. The six of us set off at night in my dad's Audi estate. I sit on my sister's lap and sleep the whole way. When I wake up, I discover the campsite where we're going to be staying for a few days.

I'm ecstatic. Time spent with my brothers is rare now. They're much older than me and they've started to lead their own lives and do their own thing. They prefer spending their holidays with friends. So this is an opportunity I need to make the most of.

After this last time we all spend together, it's just me and my parents for the holidays, but I'm a cheerful and sociable kid, and so I always manage to make friends wherever we go. I'm pretty good-natured and not what you'd call a problem child, either at home or at school. I do okay at school, although there are a few comments on my report card, 'Has ability, but spends most of his time thinking about playing football during break.' The bug is already taking hold of me.

I'm very lively and active but that doesn't mean I'm disruptive in class. That's not the way I was brought up. I respect authority. I still remember getting a clip round the ear, or a whack on the hand, to be more precise, from a teacher with some odd ideas who would make a point of doing that whenever we did something wrong. Otherwise, I'm happy to get by doing the bare minimum, with an overall average of 12 marks out of 20.

Even as a teenager, I'm pretty easy-going. A few mood swings at the most, including one time when I'm on a road trip with my parents. I'm sitting alone in the back seat, daydreaming. My dad puts the radio on to a station I don't like. I ask him to change it. He refuses. I get angry, I don't know why, and I give the car window a really hard kick. It shatters into pieces. My dad is furious and has a real go at me, as well he should. Lesson learned. I never have a tantrum like that again.

Other than this little lapse in good behaviour, I'm affectionate, sunny-natured and close to my family. I have a gang of friends that I don't manage to see very often. My schedule is just too full.

The football bug

My schooling follows the normal pattern up to year ten. I attend a secondary school near my home, while also training three evenings a week. From year 11, I begin a sports-study programme in a school in Saint-Martin-d'Hères, near Grenoble. My timetable is flexible and allows time for training. I have lessons from 8am to 3.30pm, then I go to training, a 15-minute walk away, which starts at 4pm and finishes at 6.30pm. My dad picks me up and I have just enough time to get home, do my homework, have dinner and sleep.

My life is frantic, my daily routine completely different from that of other teenagers. No going out during the week. The weekends are devoted to playing in competitions. I often have to go away on Sundays, sometimes far from home. We travel by bus.

It's exhausting. I remember leaving one morning at five o'clock to go and play a match in Cannes the same day, and returning to Grenoble straight afterwards. The next day, I went to school as usual. This is the price you pay for success, and I am willing to pay it. A life of self-denial and self-discipline for an uncertain outcome.

These sacrifices don't bother me. One year I agree to bend the rules in order to celebrate my birthday, even though I have a match the next day. My friends come and pick me up and we go for dinner at a restaurant, then on to a club. I get to bed very late. The next day I'm exhausted, but I still manage to score a hat-trick. It's as if I'm so motivated that tiredness has zero effect on me. The thought of quitting what I've started just for an easier life never once crosses my mind. I know the saying that many are called and few are chosen, but I'm tirelessly pursuing my goal. My dream.

I pass my final exams, specialising in economics and social sciences. On the day I get my results, my brother congratulates me, 'Not many young people could have done what you've managed to do during these last three years of school. You deserve a gold medal.'

I lead the life of a monk, of course, but I am not a monk. I'm starting to take a very keen interest in the opposite sex. I have a head start in this area since my first crush dates back to primary school. I must have been around eight. Her name was Aurore. She had brown hair and blue eyes. I thought she was beautiful and I promised to marry her when I grew up. Four years later, someone else took her place, and on it went.

I'm successful with girls. I'm tall and blond with blue eyes, and I'm a really nice guy, all of which is a major plus. Apparently, I'm likeable and engaging, to which I'd add that I'm a bit of a charmer, probably because of my Italian origins. I get plenty of conquests, but none of them really holds my attention. Until the day I meet the girl who will become my wife.

Jennifer.

I am 18 years old.

6

The Love of my Life

Cat and mouse

Jennifer is a year older. She lives in Saint-Martin-d'Hères and, like me, goes to Pablo-Neruda secondary school. I still live in Froges, about 12 miles or so from the school. I should never have been sent so far away, but this was the only school with a sports-study department. We are both in year 12, me specialising in economics and social science subjects and Jennifer focusing on arts and literature. I get to know her through mutual friends. We bump into each other at break times. She's pretty, and I find her different from other girls. She has a slightly

95

mysterious, distant air about her that I totally fall for. I think she likes me too, but she plays her cards close to her chest, and it's hard to interpret her expressions and the way she smiles at me. She's shy, and she's always surrounded by a gang of friends. It's not easy to approach her.

She plays football for the same club as I do, Grenoble Foot 38, and, unlike other girls, she's entirely unimpressed by aspiring footballers like me. So this advantage is no help whatsoever when it comes to trying to win her over, which doesn't make things easy for me. All the same, we're getting closer. We become friends.

An only child until the age of eight when her little sister was born, Jennifer grew up in a tight-knit family. Although both her parents work, they're always there for her. She's showered with love and attention; they take her places, they spoil her rotten. Despite this happy, privileged life, she pesters her parents to give her a little brother or sister. When Amandine arrives, her happiness is complete.

Jennifer places a lot of importance on work. Conscientious and diligent, she is often top of the class and comes home with excellent grades. She is mature for her age, with a wise head on her shoulders. She gives herself every opportunity to succeed, just as her parents did before her.

They met when they were 18. Her father lived in Dreux, her mother in Rives, a small village nearly 20 miles outside Saint-Martin-d'Hères. He moved to Grenoble out of love for his wife and because of the sports that the region offered. He was a firefighter by profession, ending his career as a crew commander. His wife worked at the main hospital in Grenoble as a medical secretary. The family lived near the fire station. Jennifer's day-to-life revolved around the fire service. She even appeared on the front page of a firefighters' calendar alongside her dad.

My in-laws are very ordinary, private people. Despite my fame, they haven't changed a bit. They avoid the media and people who want to pry into our lives.

They protect us. They always encouraged their daughter to study hard so that she would have every chance of success in life. She was brought up to value her financial independence. It's one of life's ironies that she ended up with me. But the money didn't come right away. When we first meet, I'm neither rich nor famous, quite the opposite, in fact. She has just passed her driving test and is driving her mother's little Polo. She ferries me around. At this point, I have to rely on my feet or the bus to get from A to B.

At the end of year 12, Jennifer leaves school. She changes direction and goes to a technical college to start studying for a diploma in business studies. We lose touch and I get on with my life.

I meet her again a year later, in a nightclub near Grenoble, the Phoenix Club. Every year there's a party for all those who have just passed their final exams, and we've both succeeded. I'm happy to see her again. We exchange phone numbers before we go home separately. On the way home, I find myself thinking about her. I want to see her again. The next morning, barely awake, I call her number and leave her a message. It's July. Summer. The start of the holidays.

She agrees to see me again. We're inseparable from that point on, but still just as friends. There's zero sign of any kissing on the horizon. Jennifer is not the type to throw herself into some casual fling that she doesn't think will have any future. And she's right: I'm only 18 and the thought of getting into a serious relationship scares me. I know that with her there's no way it would just be a fling, like it's been with all the others. I'm going to have to commit and I don't feel quite ready. Jennifer senses this and keeps her distance, despite our closeness.

Cupid, however, has shot his arrow. I'm attracted to her and she's attracted to me, but neither of us makes the first move. We're enjoying this little game of seduction. We allow our feelings and desire to develop. Later, she confesses that she loved me from the word go. She sensed immediately that that I was 'the one', but she was so scared of being let down that she preferred to bide her time, just observing the situation.

This waiting game is no chore for her. Jennifer is an independent woman who enjoys her own company. What with her studies, friends, family and all the sport she does, she's more than content with her lot. As she's fond of saying, she 'doesn't need a guy around'. Her life suits her perfectly just the way it is.

All the same, we spend a lot of time together. We go to the pool and the cinema. We go swimming in the lake, and wander the streets of Grenoble. We behave like a couple, except we're not. Our friends watch us with amusement. They're just waiting for the moment when one of us cracks. We're taking our time. We go our separate ways for a few days to go on holiday, then, at the start of the new term, Jennifer starts a diploma in international business studies. As for me, I'm off to university.

In September, I have a birthday party at my parents' house. Jennifer is the only girl invited. Late that evening, after she's gone home, I ask my sister Bérengère what she thinks. I want to know if she likes her, if she thinks I'd be happy with her. I have a feeling this is going to be a serious relationship and I need reassurance.

Inseparable

This little game of cat and mouse lasts a few more months, until 30 December 2004. I'm going to join my cousin in Cavaillon for a few days' holiday. Jennifer offers to take me to the station, where I'll get my bus. As we're saying goodbye, I move in close and I kiss her. We both feel a powerful surge of emotion; I know and she knows that this first kiss is just the start of what will be a long love story.

After I get back, everything moves very quickly. We're both living with our respective parents, but we're completely inseparable. Much to Jennifer's delight, her dad agrees without any hesitation that I can sleep at theirs. Her mum too, unlike mine, who is much less trusting and wants to make sure my relationship with Jen is serious. In the meantime, I sleep over at Jen's a lot. I quickly become part of her family, and she mine. Not a day goes by that I don't see her or talk to her. I miss her whenever we're apart. Other girls hold no interest for me now. I'm completely focused on her and on our relationship. She has managed to get me to commit.

At this point, I'm playing for Grenoble. A year later, I go to Istres. Jennifer has completed her diploma in international business studies and decides to take a two-year diploma in cosmetology and dermopharmacy, studying at the Faculty of Medicine and Pharmacy in the teaching hospital in Grenoble. The thought of putting her life on hold and following me never crosses her mind. Although she loves me, she insists on finishing her studies before we embark on our future together. She's cautious and doesn't want to drop everything for me.

In 2007, I move into a small apartment in Miramas, in the south of France, and I join FC Istres. For the first time in my life, I'm living alone. Unlike the majority of professional footballers who leave their families around the age of 14 to go to a football academy, I was lucky enough to play in Grenoble and got to come home every night. I avoided the wrench of leaving my parents too soon. But it's now finally time to leave the family cocoon and spread my wings.

Jennifer joins me every weekend. She now has her qualification in cosmetology and dermopharmacy and is studying to be a beautician. As part of her studies, she has to complete several work placements. She manages to find beauty salons in Istres that take her on during the holidays. We aren't officially living together, but she's gradually moving in with me. Every time she stays over, she leaves behind some more clothes and cosmetics.

Life as a couple

In 2008, I'm transferred to Tours, in Ligue 2. Now a newly qualified beautician, Jennifer agrees to follow me. We move into a lovely apartment with two bedrooms and a living room with a small open-plan kitchen. It's a cosy nest where we can enjoy life together for the first time, far away from our families. Just a few days after we arrive, Jennifer starts going round all the beauty salons. I earn a decent living, but her motto remains the same: don't be financially dependent. Two weeks later, she has a job.

Footballers' wives suffer from this image of being gold-diggers who pass their time by spending their husbands' money. Even if most of them have had to wave goodbye to their own professional ambitions, they still exist as individuals. They're often the backbone of the family. I could never accuse Jennifer of marrying me for my money. When I started earning enough for us to live on my salary alone, she insisted on continuing to work. She had no plans to spend her days with nothing to do but wait around for me.

I have wonderful memories of those two years in Tours. Life is fun and carefree. We both go to work during the day then spend the evenings together, just the two of us or with friends. As time goes by, our circle of friends grows. Jen has made friends with a few players' wives – Marion, Élodie and Claire, the trio of girl pals. There are also our neighbours, Jérôme and Julie, with whom we've struck up a friendship. Our wives and partners regularly come to see us play, then we all spend the evening together. We're happy and madly in love.

Whenever I have a day off, we go for a drive around the local area and visit the castles of the Loire Valley. I've hardly done any travelling and I've seen very little of the world, but now, thanks to Jennifer, I'm learning all about what France has to offer. Unlike me, she travelled around a lot with her sister and parents. I'm getting an idea of what else is out there to discover. Little do I imagine at this point that later on my job will let me travel the world.

In 2010, our Tours adventure comes to an end. There are a few tears from Jennifer, already nostalgic for these two years. Montpellier have approached me and I've signed for them. My ambition to play in Ligue 1 is coming together. My career is taking off.

Notting Hill

In December, we go to London for a few days between Christmas and New Year. A romantic mini-break. I only know this city through a film that I really like, *Notting Hill*.

This trip is a big thing for me. I've got a plan in mind that could make it unforgettable. I take Jennifer to a restaurant that I've chosen carefully. It's right in the heart of the Notting Hill district. We have dinner, then I suggest we go for a stroll. It's freezing cold. Jen's shivering and begging to go back to the hotel. I insist that we keep walking a bit further. She doesn't get it. I have a very specific goal in mind. We walk for ages. Finally, we arrive in front of a small house with a blue door. This legendary house is famous for being the love nest of Julia Roberts and Hugh Grant in the film.

THE LOVE OF MY LIFE

Despite the late hour and the cold, a horde of tourists are gathered around, taking shot after shot of this iconic location. We inch our way closer to the door. It's there that I ask Jennifer to marry me. It takes a few seconds for her to gather herself.

She looks at me, brimming over with emotion.

Her answer is an excited yes.

We're still living in Montpellier and Jennifer is working for a big company there. When her schedule allows, she goes to Grenoble to do all the planning for the wedding, which is scheduled to take place six months later. Whenever I can, I go with her to meet the priest who is preparing us for marriage. We both want a religious wedding.

On 4 June 2011 at 2pm, we get married under a bright blue sky at the town hall in Saint-Martin-d'Hères. I hold a bouquet of flowers for my future wife as I wait for her to arrive. When she gets out of the car, she is overwhelmed with emotion. Tears run down her cheeks. I'm feeling emotional too. After the civil ceremony, we make our way to the church. In keeping with tradition, Jen enters the church on her father's arm, me on my mother's. When the religious ceremony is over, it's time for the speeches: Bérengère, my wife's sister Amandine, my sister-in-law Denise, and finally my mum all say a few words.

A little later that evening, we go to the Golf de Bresson for the reception. It's a beautiful hotel and golf resort located in the hills of Grenoble, high in the mountains. As the evening goes on, the sky darkens, then a thunderstorm breaks out, forcing us to take shelter inside the restaurant. But nothing can spoil this moment. We sing and dance until 6am. Our mothers have secretly made a film retracing our lives, from when we were born to when we met for the first time. The montage of images is accompanied by the music of Coldplay, our favourite band. They've thought of everything, right down to the smallest detail.

In the early morning, we escape to the Château de la Commanderie, ten minutes from Grenoble, for a wedding 'night' that will last for just a few hours. At around 1pm, we join our families for brunch at Le Chavant, a Michelin-starred restaurant. A few days later, we jet off to the Maldives for a week-long honeymoon in the sun.

Professional obligations quickly take over again. We're going back to Montpellier for one season, after which we will have to decide once and for all if we're going to leave France. Arsenal want to sign me and there is absolutely no doubt that we'll say yes. Jennifer and I take stock of the past seven years, during which time we've travelled and enjoyed life without any ties. It's time for me to take my career to the next level. Now is also the time to start thinking about starting a family. Jennifer knows that this change of lifestyle will require many concessions and sacrifices on her part. She's willing to give it a go. I accept the English club's offer.

When Jennifer tells her boss that she's quitting her job, she refuses to give the real reason. She has kept her identity secret all these years and has never revealed that she was my partner, now wife. Only her close friends know. She wants to be her own person. She's so discreet that when we go out for lunch together, she gets me to wait for her a few streets away from where she works. I don't get annoyed by this. Quite the opposite, in fact: I respect and appreciate this quality in her. I know for sure that Jennifer has always really loved me, and still does, for who I am. She had no idea where destiny would take us, and I don't think I'm wrong in saying that she might have wished a different life for us. She wanted a peaceful existence in a lovely house close to our families, near Grenoble. She longed for simplicity and anonymity. Yet she has followed me and has been there for me every step of the way, in good times and bad, never leaving my side.

In July 2012, we're off to Arsenal.

Destination Arsenal

As soon as we arrive in our new city, we're looked after by Paul Irwin, a family manager the club provides for us.

He takes care of finding us an apartment, he schedules our appointments, helps us with administrative problems, deals with day-to-day logistics, finds us a 24-hour GP, and many other tasks. This man makes our life easy, and the slight apprehensiveness we feel on stepping off the plane into a country we know nothing about is quickly fading away. We are also fortunate enough to have Domenico there to help us. He is responsible for all the technical installation in our house, including the TV and wifi network. We quickly become friends with him and his wife Emilia, and they're still part of our close circle of friends today.

Newly arrived on English soil, I need to make myself available to my club and attend the required medical examinations. A few weeks earlier, Jennifer described our perfect apartment to the family manager, and now she starts viewing places to live. In the space of a day, it's a done deal: she's found our new home. A lovely two-storey duplex with a garden, in the upmarket residential area of Hampstead, in the north of the city and very close to the heath; the countryside in London.

The club doesn't pick up the tab for our home. We pay the rent in full, in the same way as we French players pay income tax on our salary in England – and we're taxed in France too if we have property there. It's important to clarify this point for everyone who imagines we're deserting France to get out of paying tax. It's just not true. What is true, however, is that abroad we can make double or even triple what we can earn at a French club (unless you play for Paris Saint-Germain, that is).

Despite our pleasant living environment, it takes a while for Jennifer to adjust to her new life. The decision to end her career in order to follow me is hard for her to come to terms with, as she has always made a point of working and earning her own money. She accepts it, but she has to adjust. At first she's bored and misses her family and friends. I, meanwhile, am spending most of my time away from home.

After we've finished moving in, Jen sometimes walks round the apartment in circles, trying to get her bearings. Inactivity weighs heavily on her, so much so that she makes a surprising decision: while we can afford to have help in the house, she refuses to hire a cleaning lady and takes care of the housework herself. Noting my surprise, she explains it in one sentence, 'It keeps me busy.' Our families visit during the two months of summer, which staves off her boredom for a while.

By the start of the season, my wife is starting to find her feet. Arsenal have an English teacher who comes to the house three times a week. The rest of the time, she roams the city, getting to know her surroundings better.

Jennifer might be suffering from inactivity, but she can do solitude very well at least. She's independent and self-sufficient. She overcomes her natural tendency to be wary and reserved, and agrees to meet some of my French team-mates and their wives. Among them are Francis Coquelin, Sébastien Squillaci and Bacary Sagna, as well as Laurent Koscielny who I played with at Tours three years before. At the time, Jennifer had really hit it off with his wife Claire, so it was only natural that they'd get together again. These four players make it easier for us to settle in. Gradually, our circle of friends is widening. We form a close friendship with Robert Pirès – from the 1998 World Cup-winning team – and his wife Jessica.

We're getting to like our London life. I'm happy at Arsenal, Jennifer is taking to it more and more each day. It's time to start thinking about us.

Jade, Evan and Aaron

At the end of May 2013, with the season barely over, we go to Grenoble to see our families. I'm on holiday and I can devote myself 100 per cent to Jennifer, who is nine months pregnant. I'm nervous about the arrival of our first child. I can't stand the sight of needles or even a drop of blood, and I'm wondering if I'll be able to handle the situation. No matter how emotionally difficult I find it, I really want to be there at the birth.

I remember every moment. On 17 June, at around eight in the morning, Jennifer wakes me. It's time to go to the hospital – the teaching hospital in Grenoble where her mum worked and where, 27 years earlier, Jen herself was born. It's a lovely day. The sky is blue, the sun barely up. I get my car and off we go. Doctors immediately take Jennifer in for tests. I wait in the corridor, anxious and impatient. A nurse comes to get me and takes me into the room. Jennifer looks calm. She tells me that the baby is not about to arrive any time soon. She gets up and asks me to go for a little stroll outside with her. We walk around the hospital grounds. I don't want to leave her side. Every moment is important to me; to us.

The day goes by and it's not until late evening that labour begins. All my fears vanish and I discover that I have it in me to be a coach. I help her, I support her. I even find myself advising her. At 1am, a cry rings out.

115

I, meanwhile, am speechless, overcome with emotion. Jade is born. There are no words to describe how I'm feeling; I won't even try.

The nurses take our daughter away to check her over. I stay with Jennifer. I'm a little dazed, but so happy.

When they bring Jade back, I hurry to take her and hold her close to me. I take off my T-shirt to do what's known as 'skin-to-skin' with my daughter and then I give her her first bottle. The tiredness is beginning to kick in, but nothing in the world will make me go home. I can't bring myself to leave my family. The hospital staff, seeing me so determined, bring me a mattress and I sleep on the floor, close to my wife and daughter.

Three years later, on 7 March 2016, Evan makes his appearance. It's not as idyllic as it was first time round: I'm working. We're right in the middle of the season. Footballers don't get paternity leave, not even one day. The manager allows us to attend the delivery – even if there's a match that day – but if there is any training or travel scheduled for the following day, we're required to be there. This is what happened with the birth of my son.

It's a planned delivery: the baby is too big, so the doctors have decided to induce labour. That morning I have to go to training, so Jennifer is on her own when she packs her suitcase and books a cab to take her to hospital. I know she has tears in her eyes as she leaves the house without me. I join her at 1pm and once again I'm lucky enough to be present at the birth. Evan is born at ten o'clock that night. When I call my manager to let him know, he congratulates me, then says, 'See you tomorrow morning at eight.'

I wait for Jennifer to go back to her room then, at two in the morning, I go away with the team. As soon as I get back, I race to the hospital to bring my son and wife home.

For Aaron, born on 25 January 2018, luck is on our side. I'm not working. I go with my wife to hospital, I'm there for the birth for the third time, and then I go home with them.

On 23 May, I go and join the French national team to start preparations for the World Cup. My son is not even four months old. He's six months when I next see him. All this time, Jennifer has been alone with our three children.

Footballer's wife

I'm aware of the sacrifices Jennifer, like all footballers' wives, makes: of the pain they sometimes go through on special occasions when having their husband there is so important; children's birthdays I can't always be there for; Christmas parties I'm not always able to enjoy with my family because of the Boxing Day tradition – all UK football clubs play on Boxing Day. I have to join my team the day before for training and an overnighter in a hotel whether we're playing at home or away. I've spent very few Christmases with my wife and children. But what affects us most of all are painful life events, such as the deaths of loved ones. When I lost three of my grandparents and Jen lost her grandmother, I couldn't go to any of the funerals, because I was playing. Jennifer couldn't go either, since she had to take care of our children.

The public can't begin to imagine how selfless footballers' wives have to be to make it as easy as possible for us to manage our careers. Looking at it from the outside, it's true that they appear to be living the dream, but this often comes at the price of being very lonely. Money isn't everything.

Jennifer is the strength of our family, its very foundation. She takes care of everything, from running the house to sorting out the children's schooling, as well as the admin side of my job. She sees to it that I'm spared the pressures and worries of everyday life so that I can concentrate and rest before matches.

Whenever my schedule allows, I focus on my children's education. I need to meet their teachers and check our eldest's homework. When I'm at home, I want to be a part of family life, to get involved in the day-to-day stuff. I like to lie down beside them and tell them bedtime stories, bath them, take them to their sporting activities, go for a walk round the park with them, introduce them to different sights, share special moments one to one or all of us together. I want to be a father who is there for them. A dad like all the other dads. I do all I can to make sure Jennifer can rely on me whenever I'm there. But her nature takes over. She keeps a watchful eye over everything and everyone. She worries about my well-being and my diet.

I wonder if my career would have been the same if I hadn't met her. The answer is definitely not. We've built what we have together. I owe my professional success to her every bit as much as to myself. She is my biggest critic and supporter. She protects me and she has my back. Whatever offers come my way, I run them past her first. Naturally cautious, she helps me be more perceptive in certain situations, especially financial ones. She has sometimes saved me from making big mistakes, as I have an unfortunate tendency to trust people too easily. She gives me advice, but then leaves the final decision up to me.

Since I've become a top-tier footballer, and now also a world champion, Jennifer has been on the alert. Outside our families, the people we've known since childhood, and our circle of close friends and colleagues, she remains vigilant if ever anyone new enters our lives. There's no shortage of people with an ulterior motive trying to get close to us.

This is the flip-side of fame. When our children went to school in London, for a long time Jennifer refused to respond to other parents who reached out, wanting to get to know her. She questions everyone's sincerity, wondering if they like her for who she is or because her name is Madame Giroud. She is all the more suspicious because on several occasions Jade and Evan have been invited to the birthday parties of children they don't know and sometimes have never even met. One day our elder daughter came home from school and said to her, 'Mummy, a boy from school is in love with me because I'm Daddy's daughter!' Jennifer had to reassure her and try to convince her that this little boy liked her because she was kind and pretty, and not because her last name was Giroud.

How can we separate the people who genuinely want to get to know us from the ones who are just fascinated by what we represent? True to character, Jennifer stays in the background for a while, observing how other parents act and behave around her. Only then will she gradually open up to those she decides have no agenda and who she feels some sort of connection with. After being on her guard for a few months, she now counts a few close friends among the mums of our children's school-mates.

Since the World Cup, family outings have been difficult, especially in France. In England we're regarded as expats. I'm not nearly as famous here as I am in our home country. I might be a world champion, but I'm a French world champion. I'm free to go to the supermarket or wander around London in peace. I don't get many fans speaking to me when I'm in a restaurant or out for a walk with my wife and kids. And if they do approach us, they do so very politely.

In France, staying anonymous is much harder. Days out with the family are sometimes disrupted by fans who want to take photos or get me to sign autographs. How can I refuse? Playing the unapproachable star is just not me, but there's more to it than that. I remember when I was a kid, how happy I felt when I got the opportunity to go and talk to a football player. So I gladly say yes to these requests, but I keep my distance in certain situations. My wife never resents it if I get stopped in the street when I'm with her. It doesn't bother her at all. She's used to it.

Fame didn't happen overnight. We gradually discovered its upsides and downsides together, when I started playing for Istres. Jennifer never imagined at the time that this fame would spread beyond our small town, extending throughout France and even crossing borders. Today, she just gets on with it. She has come to terms with the fact that it's part of my job and part of our lives. But when we get home, it's Olivier who's there with her. Her husband, and the father of her children.

7

Footballer

Working twice as hard

I've made a great life for myself by working twice as hard as anyone else. Nothing has come naturally. It's as though I was destined to only get what I wanted by battling for it. And it's through adversity that I've grown as a person.

Competition is what drives me. I need it if I'm going to get anywhere. And what's more, I've got no interest in taking the path of least resistance. It gets me too settled in my comfort zone and doesn't motivate me to push myself. Sometimes I wish everything had gone a bit more smoothly, but fate had other things in mind for me, it seems. I've wondered if I was subconsciously putting obstacles in my own path. It's the trials life throws at me that spur me on; that I can say with certainty.

I clawed my way into existence and fought to carve out a place for myself in my family. But that was only the first round of the fight. I've had something to prove throughout my whole career: that I deserved my place on the team; that I hadn't stolen someone else's spot; that I had the right to be there. There have been times I've felt that life is unfair, but I've never given up. These things were sent to try me, as they say. I think there must have been a point to them. They probably had to happen to let me develop as a person.

I've sometimes lost my starting spot to a younger or more talented player. I've been criticised and accused of being the main reason Karim Benzema got dropped from the national team. Questions were asked about whether I should have been part of the 2018 World Cup squad at all after I failed to score, and that's before we even mention the 2019/20 season at Chelsea.

Episodes like this have marked my career, and they've really tested me. Other players might have given up or become discouraged. Not me. These low points have simply fuelled my determination, and my self-confidence has never once taken a hit. I've always wanted to believe that anything is possible and that I'd get there in the end.

A family affair

If life hadn't got in the way, it would have been my brother Romain here instead of me. His future as a footballer was all mapped out.

Like me, he starts his career at Froges, then moves to ES Manival, the best youth club in the region. Like me, he gets scouted by Grenoble Foot 38 and plays there for two years. But the similarities end there. He's spotted when he's very young and gets signed up by AJ Auxerre, the best football academy in France, with the legendary head coach Guy Roux in charge. I often go with my parents to visit Romain, and the four of us watch the pro match together. I like to go and see his room at the training academy, then we all have lunch in town. I'm proud of my brother.

Romain is called up for the French youth squad alongside Thierry Henry, Nicolas Anelka and David Trezeguet. Two out of the three will be world champions in 1998. At under-17 level, he's one of the best in the position of central defender. Time after time he's selected for the national youth team.

My brother reaches great heights very quickly. But the world of football is ruthless. Despite his undeniable talent, he falls victim to the subjective opinions and the decisions of a manager who no longer wants him. Romain loses his place at Auxerre and takes it very badly. Out of pride, or because he can't stand what he sees as injustice, he rebels and shoots himself in the foot by behaving inappropriately towards his managers.

Childhood

❶ : Two years old, and already
   passionate about football. © DR

❷ : In my parents' house in Froges (1993). © DR

❸ : At the Froges Olympique Club. © DR

❹ : With my mother in the kitchen. (1995). © DR

❺ : In my grandparents' apartment
   in Val-d'Isère (1997). © DR

❻ : One of my first cups. © DR

❼ : On my tenth birthday, with my mother. © DR

Family

Top, left: Marriage of my brother Romain (2002). © DR

Top right: On my 18th birthday, with my brothers. © DR

Centre: With my brothers and my sister (October 2014). © DR

Opposite: With my father (summer 2014). © DR

Top left :
My marriage to Jennifer (2011). © DR

Top, right: Puskas Prize for the most beautiful goal of the year (2017). © DR

Above: First family ski vacation in Courchevel (2020). © DR

Opposite: Christmas in London (2019). © DR

Grenoble

Grenoble Foot 38 (2006). © DR

Tours

On tour with Laurent Koscielny (2008). © DR

Left and top: 2012, year of the French title win (2012). The three photos are taken at the Mosson stadium in Montpellier. © DR

Below: Celebrating the Ligue 1 title on the Place de la Comédie in Montpellier (2012). © DR

Arsenal

Top, left: With Jade (2014). © DR

Top, right: Treble against Olympiakos, pride of my coach Arsene Wenger (2015). © Stuart MacFarlane/Arsenal FC/Getty Images

Bottom left: FA Cup (2017). © Stuart MacFarlane/Arsenal FC/Getty Images

Bottom right: FA Cup Final (2017). © DR

Centre: Scorpion kick (2017). © Shaun Botterill/Getty Images/AFP

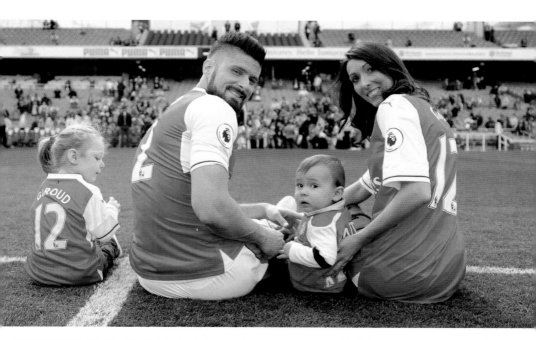

Top: With Jen, Jade and Evan, on the pitch at Emirates Stadium (2017). © DR

Bottom: Celebration. © Stuart MacFarlane/Arsenal FC/Getty Images

2018 World Cup

© Matthias Hangst/Getty Images/AFP

All photos with the World Cup are taken on 15 July 2018, the evening of the final at the Luzhniki Stadium in Moscow.

© Xavier Laine/Getty Images

He admits it himself. He rejects offers from clubs he doesn't consider to be up to his standard. At the time, agents aren't so much of a thing, and so he has to manage his professional future on his own, without any advice or support whatsoever. He chooses to hang up his boots.

I'm 13 years old and watching things unfold from a distance. I don't completely understand the situation, but seeing how my parents react, I realise that this abrupt end to things is just as painful for them as it is for my brother. They perceive it as a failure. My dad does a lot of soul-searching. Although he has been very involved in Romain's career, he's now wondering if he was there for him enough. Dad regrets not having done something more about it when Romain was first having a hard time.

This shattered dream takes its toll on the whole family.

My brother bounces back quickly, however, getting a diploma in dietetics and becoming a dietitian and nutritionist. He found his vocation and has no regrets. He has learned to love football and enjoy watching matches again, after a long period during which he turned his back on the whole scene. Now, he lives out his passion through me.

He has never shown the slightest hint of bitterness or jealousy towards me. Quite the opposite, in fact. It's now his turn to be proud of his kid brother, although he's definitely hard to please. Extremely hard to please, in fact.

He doesn't think twice about piling the pressure on and regularly has a real go at me, 'Oli, get your foot off the brake.' He wants to get it through to me that I have to give my all, get out of my comfort zone, keep raising the bar higher. I'm fearful of what he thinks of me and what comments he's going to make after every match. Looking back, I know the fact that he's so hard on me has served me well at key moments in my career. Romain has wanted me to succeed where he failed.

A fledgling footballer

Life as a fledgling footballer continues. It's an unforgettable period in my life. I play with two of my best friends, twins Damien and Johann. We grew up together. I'm five when I join the club at Froges, playing first as an under-seven, then an under-nine, an under-11 and continuing through. The last thing on my mind is making a career of this. All I want to do is to play football with my mates and be like my brother: wearing the same bracelet on my wrist, getting a massage after the match. Sometimes my muscles ache. My gran massages me as best she can to relieve the pain and I say to her, 'Grandma, do you realise how lucky Romain is? He can get a massage whenever he wants!'

My ambition goes no further that that. What matters to me is showing off my talents to my family and friends when they come to watch me play. Everything I aspire to can be summed up in two words: score goals.

I'm a good player, maybe one of the best on my team, and I seem to have a natural talent. I'm developing skills as a forward – although I sometimes have to moonlight as a defender if the managers ask me to step in when we're a player short. I score goals, but I'm not a boy wonder. No one is really pinning their hopes on me. When I later go on to lift the World Cup, my managers at Froges say my success is down to strength of character more than technique. As far as they're concerned, it's my mindset that got me there. I'm not sure I entirely agree with them.

I've always been passionate and headstrong, with a dogged determination to win. At secondary school, I take part in inter-class tournaments. I'm ready to give absolutely everything I can on the pitch because I can't stand the thought of losing. If we are ever defeated, I'm in tears. I only play to win. I'm a competitor through and through, but my success isn't down to this alone.

Romain already believes in me. He spotted my potential in a match against Grenoble. I'm eight years old. I've only been playing for a few minutes when I score an unbelievable goal on the volley. My brother and dad are watching the match. At the final whistle, Romain comes up to me, 'Now I know you're a striker, a goalscorer. You've got it in your blood.'

It's down to me and me alone to make the most of my abilities. It's still too early, though. I'm not mature enough yet to launch myself into a professional career. But I live and breathe football from morning to night. I'm a diehard France supporter and a massive fan of Zinedine Zidane, whose posters are all over my bedroom walls. I grew up supporting Marseille, where Jean-Pierre Papin, one of my favourite players, and Didier Deschamps, my future manager, both cut their teeth, winning the prestigious Champions League in 1993. I also admire the Brazilian player Ronaldo. He's an inspiration to all kids my age. I never get tired of watching videos of the Dutchman Marco van Basten, but my absolute idol is the Ukrainian Andriy Shevchenko, who plays for the brilliant AC Milan. He can score in all positions, with his right foot, his left foot, his head – a genius, basically. I take a lot of inspiration from this player, to the point where I secretly imitate him when I'm warming up and jogging. I try to copy his movements and his style of running, but my natural way of doing things quickly takes over. I am not Shevchenko.

At the end of the season, during a training match, I'm spotted in my small village by scouts from the Grenoble Foot 38 club. I'm 12 years old at this point. They decide to give me a trial, which turns out to be successful. I'm proud and happy. But after the initial elation has worn off, a feeling of doubt creeps in and questions start going round and round my head. 'Is there any point in going? This sport requires enormous sacrifice – is it all worth it? Many are called but few are chosen.' There is no guarantee that I will be successful and be able to turn professional.

My brother's failure pursues me like a shadow, holding me back. I'm scared the same thing will happen to me. But I have a real opportunity here, and I'm going to have to take it with both hands, no matter how things eventually pan out. Grenoble is the flagship club in the region. I'm just a kid, though, and my friends are still my top priority. I'm naive and innocent. Immature. Not without some misgivings, I decide I'm going to have to tell my pals the news. I pluck up the courage to ask them, 'Do you think I should leave you here and go to Grenoble?' Their replies are unanimous. 'Just go! What are you even hesitating for? We'd all give anything to be in your shoes! Go for it!'

My parents don't get too involved. They've had their fingers burnt by Romain's unfortunate experience, and so they neither encourage me nor try to stand in my way. They're in a tricky situation. On the one hand they're scared I might fail, the chances of success in this profession being so low. But on the other hand, they can't stop me from giving it my best shot. All they can do is warn me about possible disappointment further down the line. It's up to me to take the risk or not. I decide to give it a go. That way I can never regret not having tried.

Grenoble Foot 38

I join Grenoble Foot 38, which comes with the not insignificant perk of being able to come home every night. Settling in at my training club is not that easy. My team-mates see me as the little country boy who has just landed in the big city, which earns me a few unpleasant remarks. My friends Alexis Lafon and Christophe Lautier, also from a small village, are the butt of the same joke. I have to stand up for myself, even though my heart's in my boots just thinking about it. I can't let them walk all over me or I'm going to get picked on by everyone. The new recruits suffer the same fate every year. It's a kind of initiation ceremony that lasts as long as it lasts and involves winding us up in the dressing room or minutes before a match, just to test us. Woe betide us if we display any weakness. At that age, we show each other no mercy. If we can't think of a good comeback, we resort to using our fists. Anything goes when it comes to fitting in and earning respect.

I'm slowly but surely finding my niche. I come to be accepted by the group. At this level, the aim isn't to turn professional or to make a lot of money, but even so, the coaches demand a lot of us and a competitive spirit emerges, with its fair share of rivalries and dirty tricks. Friendship takes a back seat; everyone is out for themselves. I have to make a name for myself and fight to earn the right to play, and put my scruples aside when I'm asked to take someone else's place on the team or, conversely, swallow my pride when I 'keep the bench warm'. I keep things in perspective, take what comes to me with a sense of detachment and don't put any pressure on myself.

A bankable name

There's nothing insurmountable about the problems I'm facing at this stage. This is just the beginning. The real pressure starts much later, once I become a bankable name, first at Montpellier, then when I sign for Arsenal and Chelsea. At this point, I suddenly find myself in a whole new world, one where money talks. As the financial stakes get higher, so the pressure intensifies. The higher our salaries, the greater the demands on us. My level of commitment has to be on a par with my earnings.

By commitment, I mean my performance and my requirement to get results. Our transfer fees increase according to our showings on the pitch. This money goes directly into the club's coffers and is reinvested into the purchase of other players. And besides, it's easier to negotiate a higher salary when several clubs are expressing an interest.

There's no mercy for a player who's in poor shape. Managers don't care about the individual. For them, it's all about the group. Their objective is to build a winning team. Twice a year, during the transfer window, players are put on the market to be sold, bought or loaned. We are commodities, quite simply because we have a market value, which varies according to our performance and our age.

We are the property of a club that pays our wages, and we have to respect every single clause in the contract we've signed; our commitments to our sponsors, for example. We're required to take part in any marketing events requested by the kit manufacturer: ads, interviews, photo shoots, and so on. The brand exploits our image and owns part of the rights. Being selected for the national team makes this even more the case.

Before each international competition, one full day is devoted to the various sponsors, with everyone filming adverts and videos or attending photo shoots and interviews. We're not allowed to say no.

As well as the prestige attached to the national team, advertising contracts and TV broadcasting rights generate astronomical revenues. Professional football, while traditionally a working-class game, is the most widely played sport in the world and gets the most media coverage, hence the mind-boggling sums of money flying around that serve to tarnish its image. We have to remember its positive side, which is that it unites millions of people of all backgrounds and social classes. The beautiful game breaks down the barriers created by society and allows people to experience extraordinary emotions.

In addition to the obligations imposed on us by our club, we also sign a personal contract with a kit sponsor, which requires us to wear the brand in question when we're interviewed on TV or during a photo shoot, and in our day-to-day lives too. It's essential that footballers surround themselves with the right people to look after the financial side of things, such as negotiating our contracts, and to manage our image. This is where agents have a role to play. Choosing the right one, not being blinded by promises that can be easily made and just as easily broken, is a real headache. What criteria should you use when making the decision to trust one over another?

The world of agents is one where there is no shortage of sharks. Some of them can smell an opportunity to hit the jackpot. It can all get out of hand in a variety of ways: insane fees, conflicts of interest, secret alliances with managers and directors, bribes and backhanders – I could go on. Not all agents are crooks and there's no denying their skills. They're indispensable. What's crucial is to establish a relationship with your agent that's built on mutual trust. This partnership must have a single objective in its sight: professional success. We have to be extremely vigilant when it comes to choosing the person who is going to look after our careers and our financial interests. The profession is poorly regulated and the few rules that do exist are easy to break. Fortunately, I have never had a bad experience with an agent.

When I first start out in football, my brother keeps an eye on me. Never leaving my side, he gives me advice on the game itself and on how I should conduct myself. It's Romain who talks to the directors of Grenoble Foot 38 when I decide to leave Froges. He knows all about the inner workings of this industry and he protects me.

Later, when I turn pro, I decide to put my career in the hands of agents. I don't want to mix family and business. Garo Khachikian is my first agent. I'm playing for Grenoble Foot 38 and he comes to Créteil to see a match between the two teams, in the hope, I imagine, of spotting one or more gold nuggets, as you might call them. After the game, he lets me know he's interested. He's young and doesn't have a lot of experience in the industry. Romain and I talk to him. He seems honest, and so we decide to work with him. I don't have much choice, frankly. My career has barely got off the ground and agents aren't exactly queueing up to offer me their services.

Two years later, I meet Guillaume, who comes to see me in Marseille. His pitch comes across as convincing. I want to take things up a notch. I stop working with Garo, but we keep in touch and exchange news from time to time.

In 2008, I sign up with this new agent and his associates. Guillaume and Alain are based in Montpellier. The other two, Michaël and Pascal, are in Menton. Between them, they manage the careers of several players in Ligue 1 and abroad. To start with, when I'm playing for Montpellier, I work with Guillaume and Alain. Michaël, who speaks several languages and has a wide network of contacts, then takes over when I arrive at Arsenal. My agents are assisted by Giselle, a wonderful person who managed my assets for ten years. I was very fond of her. She was caring and protective of me, and I very soon counted her among my close friends. Sadly, Giselle passed away in 2019. I'll never forget her.

Michaël and I work well together. My strong performance on the pitch makes his job easier. This in no way detracts from his expertise, because he still has to take care of the hardest task of all: negotiating my contracts as skilfully as possible. We've been working together for 13 years now, in a relationship based on complete and mutual trust. I am very close to Michaël.

Not there just to make up the numbers

Let's return to the start of my career. When I'm 12 years old, these high-level concerns are a long way off.

I'm playing with the under-13 team in the regional league.

At 14, I win a French championship title with the Rhône-Alpes team. I'm not in the starting line-up and on average, I only play in every other match. One day my trainer, Richard Boilon, comes up to me, 'You've got good skills in front of the goal – you're a natural striker, a goalscorer. But you also have this ability to read the game faster than the others. That's important.' This information comes as a revelation. I gain in self-confidence and I realise that I'm not there just to make up the numbers.

Richard has played a significant role in my career. As well as the purely football-related aspects of the job, he made it his mission to pass on to us values such as respect and humility. One story in particular comes to mind. The team is leaving for an away game and Richard is already on the bus by the time I get on. I don't know if my mind is busy with something else or if I just haven't noticed he's there but, anyway, I forget to say hello to him. In a tone that signals that he is not impressed by this, he calls me out in front of the team, 'Are you not saying hello, then? Not going to shake my hand either?' The implication being: who do you think you are? I'm annoyed with myself and apologise. That day, I realise the importance of hierarchy in sport and the respect I owe my coaches as well as my team-mates. Saying hello and shaking hands seems an obvious thing to do. These marks of respect are typically French. In England, even getting a simple hello is far from guaranteed.

Around the same time, Auxerre have been discreetly reaching out to me to try to persuade me to join their prestigious training academy. My friend and team-mate Alexis Lafon has also been approached. 'Come with me,' he says. 'It'll be easier to settle in if we're both there.' My family normally take a back seat, but this time they step in, 'You're too young and too immature! You're not going!' I don't push the point. It's true that Alexis is a lot more mature than me. And anyway, this club, ironically enough, is none other than the same one that shattered my brother Romain's dreams. Saying yes is out of the question.

I stay at Grenoble Foot 38 and continue my budding career with the under-15s. I'm starting to play against the big boys, like Marseille, Saint-Étienne and Lyon. At 17, I sign a professional training contract, which Romain negotiates for me, then I join the reserve team. My career takes another turn. There is more at stake now. The game is becoming more serious, the competition too. I'm no longer playing football just to have a laugh with my friends. Now it's about winning titles and developing as a player. I'm beginning to hope, to believe in myself, and in my dream of becoming a professional footballer. All the more so given that there aren't many of my under-13 and under-15 team-mates left. Most of them are no longer in the running. But I'm still here.

I deserve to be here, but every day I realise that I can't ever take that for granted, and nor should I. Football is an endless cycle of starting all over again, and that means we need to keep re-evaluating ourselves, stay vigilant, and always strive to do better. The trophies, prestigious as they are, don't change that. They represent the end result of our work at a specific point in time, the reward for years of effort, but they don't make us immune to failure.

Aware of just how fragile my place on the team is, I hang in there and keep grafting. In 2005, when I'm playing for the reserve team, rumours start to circulate about two or three players – me being one of them – who are likely to sign a professional contract. The holy grail. Bernard Blaquart, the director of the training academy and the reserve team manager, lets us know we stand a good chance.

More motivated than ever, I get off to a decent start in the season, but I'm stopped in my tracks by a serious problem with my lateral meniscus. Surgery is unavoidable. This sudden halt to proceedings puts my immediate future and my chances of signing a professional contract in jeopardy, but there's nothing I can do about it. I have three months of enforced rest after which I gradually resume training. I struggle to get back into it and I'm in pain, but I fight hard and try to give it my all. Towards the end of the season, the head coach feels I'm ready and asks me to play again. There aren't many matches left so I have few opportunities to prove myself. Fortunately, I'm not kept in suspense for too long. Bernard comes to talk to me. I'll never forget his words, 'The club is going to offer you a professional contract.'

It's one of the happiest days of my life. The first great memory of my football career. I'm 19, and in a few weeks' time I'll be a professional footballer.

Turning pro

I sign a three-year contract in Max Marty's office. He's the sporting director of Grenoble Foot 38. My salary will be €2,500 a month for the first year. Romain is by my side. I'll be wearing the number 22 shirt with my name printed on it.

Once the contract has been signed, I need to get out there and play. The first year isn't easy. I score two goals in 17 matches and only start twice. I'm on the fringes, competing with players who are much more experienced than me, and I'm only on the pitch for a few minutes at a time. It's hard to get any opportunity to stand out and to show Yvon Pouliquen, my manager, what I'm capable of in the first team. I wait restlessly on the bench, but I have to grin and bear it. I'm biding my time. I make up for this lack of minutes by playing regularly with the reserve team. I score plenty of goals and I'm one of the top scorers in the fourth tier, which gives my self-confidence a boost.

On 26 February 2007, my efforts pay off. I score my first professional goal at the Lesdiguières Stadium in Grenoble in a match against Le Havre, getting the ball past a certain Steve Mandanda, who I'd go on to meet again some years later when we both play for France. I've been waiting for this moment for a whole year. Grenoble are losing 1-0 when the manager brings me on.

In the 85th minute, my team-mate Steven Pelé equalises. Then, in the last minute, I win possession and score; 2-1 to Grenoble. I'm over the moon. I'm the hero who has stepped in and secured victory for his team.

The following year, my honeymoon period at the club suffers a setback with the arrival of a new manager, Mécha Baždarević, who wants to keep me in his squad but leave me on the bench. I'm not happy with this decision. Once again, I'm not going to get enough game time and therefore not enough visibility. It's becoming apparent that if I stay with this team, I'm not going to get any opportunities to progress. I'm not my manager's first choice.

Although I'm still under contract for two years, I ask him to let me go. The negotiations are tough, but I don't let myself get intimidated. I have to really push my point and use all the arguments I have at my disposal to get him to change his mind. Meanwhile, Garo, my agent at the time, is scrambling to find me a club. He tells me that Istres are interested. I can't make up my mind about this. Istres previously played in Ligue 2 but have been relegated to the National Championship

League, i.e. the third division. They are no longer part of the professional leagues, although they will retain their professional status for two years.

It's a difficult decision to make. Go back down to a third division club and be sure of playing, or stay in Grenoble and spend more time on the bench than on the pitch? Dilemma. I pray, I ponder, I weigh up the pros and cons. A few days later, Nassim Akrour, one of my Grenoble Foot 38 team-mates, gets a call from the chairman of FC Istres, Bertrand Benoît, who's after some information about me. Nassim tells the chairman straight that he should sign me, then he comes to see me. In a few words, he sways my decision. 'Olivier,' he says, 'if you stay in Grenoble, the manager is not going to let you play, and that's that. You won't get the opportunities, whereas in Istres you'll have the chance to show what you can do. You'll be able to develop your own personality as a player and really progress.'

I call my agent to tell him that I want to join FC Istres. I am loaned to the club for a period of one year.

Istres

By signing for Istres, I move up the social ladder to a point beyond my wildest dreams. I'm bringing in a salary of €8,000 a month. Along with this change in status comes independence. For the first time, I'm living alone, doing my own shopping and learning how to cook. With my driving licence under my belt, I treat myself and buy my mum's cousin's Polo; my first car, which spells freedom. I fly the nest. Jennifer joins me whenever she can.

This new life does a lot for my confidence and I make my mark at my new club pretty fast. Despite an injury that causes me to miss part of the season, I perform well against experienced players, scoring 14 goals in 33 games.

At the end of the season, I'm contractually required to return to Grenoble, who in the meantime have moved up to Ligue 1, but I understand that Baždarević still doesn't want me in the first team. He has signed other strikers and sees me as a reserve. I pile on the pressure to be allowed to leave. Baždarević refuses, then snaps, 'You're not good enough to play in Ligue 2, never mind Ligue 1.' Maybe he's right, but let's not forget that he's not giving me any opportunity to show any potential talent I do have. His words sting, but I don't let myself get discouraged by being written off so early, and I vow I'll prove him wrong.

Four years later, in a match between Montpellier, where I'm playing at the time, and Baždarević's new club, Sochaux, I get my chance. Raring to go and with fire in my belly, I'm not going to rest until I've proved to him that he made a huge mistake. I power my team to the top of the league table by scoring a hat-trick. In the post-match interview, Baždarević sums it up in one sentence, 'Giroud is an exceptional player.'

Frédéric Arpinon, the head coach at FC Istres, asks his superiors to push things through faster by buying out the last year of my contract with Grenoble. It will cost €150,000, a sum that the club can well afford. What I don't know at that point is that another club has spotted me: Tours FC. The club's directors are super efficient, and super motivated too, it seems, as they pounce faster than FC Istres.

Tours

It's 2008 and I'm off for new adventures with Tours, a Ligue 2 team. The icing on the cake is that once again I get to see Max Marty, the former director of Grenoble Foot 38, with whom I signed my first professional contract. Max is now the sporting director of my new club.

Pumped and full of confidence, I have a good first season. I play alongside Laurent Koscielny, who I meet again a few years later at Arsenal and then again when we play for France. I'm unstoppable. After training, I stay on the pitch to practise volleys and other set-pieces in front of goal. I'm still on the pitch when my mates are already out of the shower.

My second season is even better. On 18 September 2009, during a fixture against Arles-Avignon, I score four goals. I feel invincible. I score 23 goals in 40 games and I'm named top goalscorer. I win the National Union of Professional Footballers Ligue 2 Player of the Year trophy. Year by year my salary increases until I'm earning €15,000 a month.

At the end of the season, the phone starts ringing. Several clubs are interested in me: Montpellier and Monaco, but also Celtic and Middlesbrough. My agents are working flat out to get me the best contract at the best club. My preference is Celtic and their legendary stadium, Celtic Park, with its 60,000 capacity, is the stuff of dreams. I can already see myself there. Strategically, this club would be a great springboard to realise my ambition to eventually play in the English Premier League.

In the meantime, Alain and Guillaume, my agents in Montpellier, come up with the idea of approaching Louis Nicollin, the now much-missed chairman of the Montpellier Hérault Sport Club team. They advise me to take his call, 'You're free to decide which club you want to play for, but you should listen to what the Montpellier chairman wants to say.' Flattered that this legend of French football wants to talk to me, I agree. Listening to him, I realise just how much his club wants me. Straight off, he says, 'What are you gonna do over there in Scotland in Kilchmarchnock?' Mentioning the town of Kilmarnock is a slightly roundabout way of badmouthing the whole Scottish championship. The chairman is desperate to persuade me not to sign with Celtic, who at this point are top of my list. 'Come to us, you'll be all right, you'll be happy.' He explains his club's strategic plan in detail. His star striker, the French-Colombian Victor Hugo Montaño, has left the club, and Nicollin assures me that I'll take over as number one striker. I'm becoming more and more tempted by his offer. I end the call after asking him if I can think about it for a little while, but I already know that my future lies with his club.

The next day, my agents come to see me with the financial offers from the various clubs that are interested, including Celtic and Middlesbrough, who are offering me twice as much as Montpellier. At no point do Alain and Guillaume use this as an argument to try and persuade me to move abroad. Quite the opposite, in fact. Instead, they say, 'Would you not like to leave your mark in Ligue 1 in France before you head overseas?' It's a good argument.

Montpellier

On 1 July 2010, I sign for three years with Montpellier. The demands on me crank up a notch. I'm expected to get results. The chances to score come less often and are less easy: we're up against some excellent players. It's top-flight football. The pressure is intense. We're in the spotlight, playing in packed stadiums. I discover the press and how critical it can be. Heaped with praise one day, crucified the next. I gradually get used to it.

My first season is an adjustment period and not entirely successful. I only score 14 goals in 43 games, but René Girard, the head coach, has faith in me. It's not until my second year there that I really go for it. Our team is made up of a mixture of experienced and young players. I'm 25, somewhere in between the two generations. The chemistry among the players is working like a dream and our manager really knows how to get us fired up and hungry to win. I score a hat-trick against Sochaux, then another one against Dijon. I'm working tirelessly and my efforts are paying off. Everything I try seems to work and I feel like I can walk on water. My salary is soaring – I bring in nearly €50,000 a month during the first year – and so is my reputation.

Jennifer and I rent a lovely house with a swimming pool in Lattes, an area on the outskirts of Montpellier near the beach. We're finally living the dream: sea, sun and success. I'm the top scorer in Ligue 1 across the season. With 25 goals notched up in 42 games, I'm one of the main men behind my team winning the league title for the first time in their history.

I'm not letting either my growing fame or the money go to my head. I don't go crazy. The way I was brought up is still a deeply rooted part of who I am and it stops me from going overboard. I'm not flashing my cash around either; I'm putting money aside. That's not to say that I don't spoil Jennifer and give us a comfortable life. We don't go without, it's just that we don't spend money like water.

Every year the French footballers' union organises sessions to warn us about this. 'Put some of your earnings aside,' they advise us, 'because a career in football lasts on average just seven years. Don't squander your money.' I don't need this advice – my mum told me the same thing years ago. Right from when I first started earning, I've been investing in bricks and mortar to give us something to fall back on, just in case.

Arsenal

Onwards and upwards. After two great years in Montpellier, it's time to set my sights further afield and on the international stage. I've made history in French football. I now have to distinguish myself elsewhere and show what I'm capable of as part of a major European team.

For several months now, Arsenal have been keeping a close eye on me. At the end of the 2012 season my agents let me know that they are interested in me. This is the club I've always dreamt of playing for. As well as being so prestigious, Arsenal have also been home to some legends of French football, like Robert Pirès, Thierry Henry, Patrick Vieira, Emmanuel Petit and many others. Not forgetting Arsène Wenger, who over the years has become an Arsenal icon. I discuss all this with my agent Michaël, and ask him to examine their offer carefully. Other clubs approach me, but Arsenal is my first choice. I want to play there. I want to be a Gunner! The financial transactions take a while. My transfer fee is said to be in the region of £13m.

Meanwhile, I get called up to the France squad to play in Euro 2012. I stay focused on the tournament, but at the same time I'm keeping a close eye on developments on the other side of the Channel. I'm looking forward to the outcome. To my surprise, this happens when our wives visit our base camp one day. I'm happy to see Jennifer again. A little smile plays on the corner of her lips. She opens her bag and hands me a document. 'All you've got to do is sign on the dotted line,' she says. Michaël has given her the job of bringing me the finalised contract, four years, which binds me to the legendary club Arsenal, where I'll see my friend Laurent Koscielny again. I'm overjoyed. Another dream has come true, and one of the biggest of all.

On 26 June 2012, I'm officially wearing the number 12 red and white jersey. I discover Colney, Arsenal's training ground in north London, just half an hour from our home in Hampstead.

The boss, Arsène Wenger, is revered because he has taken the club to a top-four finish in the Premier League every year he's been in charge. Wenger campaigned for this modern training centre which boasts excellent facilities, enabling players to do their best possible work.

There's a huge gym just past reception on the left, and a restaurant upstairs where we can have breakfast or lunch.

I'm impressed with the size of the dressing rooms and all the different equipment in the treatment room. I'll enjoy going there after training to get looked after by the masseurs and physios. There is also a large swimming pool, a jacuzzi, sauna, steam room and an ice bath to speed up our recovery. Looking round everywhere, it hits me that I've just signed for one of Europe's top clubs. My eyes are shining and I feel like a little kid again seeing the photos of all the big Arsenal stars lining the walls. The manager watches me, smiling, then says, 'There you go, you're a Gunner now too. And remember, you're here because you deserve to be.' His words make it clear that he has complete confidence in me. However, the ball is in my court. It's up to me and me alone to make my mark here.

Wenger is passionate about his job and his love for beautiful football is unconditional. He watches players closely and can immediately detect each one's individual talent. But beyond that, he can also spot a player's ability to read a game and adapt his style of play to Arsenal's core principles, which are all about teamwork and possession of the ball.

Being a good player is no guarantee of victory, though, and Wenger is well aware of this. That is why, if one of us is going through a rough patch, he is always there, showing a tremendous capacity to be positive and encouraging at all times so that the player finds his confidence again. This quality of his really left its mark on me and helped me a lot at certain points in my life. The two of us formed a bond based on a mutual respect for each other's background. I admired where he had come from as well as what he had done for the club in terms of increasing its influence and reputation on the world stage. On his side, he always made a point of reminding me of the road he'd travelled to get to where he was. Something he still does.

The season gets under way, and I discover a whole new world of football with a completely different atmosphere. Unlike in French stadiums, there is no kop. Instead, the thousands of fans are spread out around the stadium and sing in unison throughout the match. I've never experienced an atmosphere like it. Now that stringent security measures have got rid of the hooligans, we can play with complete peace of mind. The stands are located right on the edge of the pitch. Being so close to the supporters gives us a real boost. Despite their passion and enthusiasm, they always behave with respect.

There are fans of all ages. I've seen old ladies inside the stadium with their faces painted in club colours, wearing football shirts and singing at the top of their lungs. In England, this sport is a celebration, a religion, a legacy passed down from generation to generation. The fans are as demanding as they are passionate. What they expect from us is spectacle, so-called champagne football, and results. I have to get used to a whole different way of playing, one that's much more athletic and that demands a level of physical effort on the pitch that's way tougher than anything in France. We move from one penalty area to another and we're always on the attack, unlike French or Italian play, which tends to favour a more tactical game plan. This all takes some getting used to.

I remember my first home game at the Emirates Stadium, against Sunderland. It's a very emotional moment for me as I've put on the legendary red and white jersey for the first time. The score is 0-0 when I come on in the 65th minute. I'm longing to score the winner for my team, but as it turns out, I'll need to wait a few more weeks before I net my first goal. Next up is a memorable match at Anfield. The manager starts me, and although I prove worthy of his faith in me, I don't manage to get a goal. We win 2-0, and I'm delighted by the final score, but another great thing happens that I never saw coming. A chant goes up in the crowd to the tune of 'Hey Jude' by The Beatles. A chant using my name that fans wrote for me. Even today, I'm overcome with emotion when I think back to that moment. What a sense of pride I have. A sense of gratitude too. This match marks the start of a special relationship between the Arsenal fans and me.

On 26 September 2012, I finally score my first goal for the Gunners, in a League Cup match against Coventry. Having been slipped in on goal by a pass from my friend Francis Coquelin, I fire the ball over the keeper's head and into the net. What a weight off my shoulders. I've been so looking forward to this moment. This gives my confidence a real boost and I do it again a week later, scoring the equaliser in a Premier League match at West Ham. My brothers are in the stands watching and this really lifts my spirits. It's the first time they've been to London since I moved here. There's no doubt that knowing they're nearby is giving me added motivation and strength. We win the match 3-1 and I go out to celebrate with my brothers over a few beers.

My season has really begun now. I feel good, both on and off the pitch, helped by all the supportive people who work at the club. This first Premier League season, 2012/13, has been a pretty successful adjustment period for me, with 17 goals and seven assists notched up in 46 games. But deep down I know I can do better.

The following season gets off to a strong start. On 1 September 2013 I score an important goal in the north London derby against Tottenham. It's the only goal of the match and gives us a long-awaited derby victory. I make a run to the near post and receive a through ball, which I sneak past the eagle eye of my friend and Spurs goalkeeper Hugo Lloris with the outside of my left foot. This goal boosts my standing with Arsenal supporters and, as my third goal in three Premier League matches, continues my impressive start to the season.

In June 2014 I'm called up to the national team to play in the World Cup in Brazil. We're knocked out in the quarter-finals by Germany. I then rejoin my team-mates who are already in pre-season training. Several of us international players have missed the start of preparations because we didn't get our summer break until after the World Cup. Nevertheless, on 10 August 2014 the boss puts me on the team sheet for the

Community Shield match. We're playing Manchester City. With only a few days' training behind me, I don't feel physically ready. But I'm a born competitor and nothing is going to make me miss out on playing in a final at the legendary Wembley, the fifth biggest stadium in the world. The manager brings me on and very quickly I score a superb goal with a curling shot into the top corner. As it happens, City's goalkeeper is Willy Caballero, who I end up meeting again at Chelsea four years later. We win the match 3-0 and lift another trophy, my second with Arsenal in the space of three months. The season is going well already.

I still have to catch up on training, and I start the first two Premier League matches on the bench. The second of these will end up being a career-changer. On 23 August we play away to Everton. The atmosphere is electric, which is no bad thing as far as I'm concerned. Losing 2-0 at half-time, Arsène Wenger decides to bring me off the bench. I equalise for my team in the 89th minute with a header from a Nacho Monreal cross.

I'm over the moon, the supporters are out of their seats giving me a standing ovation, and amid the applause I hear them singing 'my song'. I'm finally back and ready for this new season.

Stoppage time seems to last an eternity, but we hang in there. A few seconds before the final whistle, during a completely innocuous passage of play, I take a knock after a defender's clearance and feel a sharp pain in my ankle. I decide to stay on the pitch anyway. I'm limping, but I'm not too worried. I'm thinking I must just have twisted it. When I get back to the dressing room, the pain gets worse. It really hurts. The next morning, I go to the medical centre to get it X-rayed, just for a bit of reassurance.

The medic Gary O'Driscoll, a brilliant man, summons me and quietly gives me the result, 'Oli, I don't have good news. You have a clean fracture of the medial malleolus of your left ankle.'

I haven't yet grasped how serious this is. The only thing that matters to me is how long I'll be out for.

'About three months,' he replies.

I'm absolutely gobsmacked. Just yesterday I was the hero of the match, brimming with confidence and all set for the coming weeks, and now I have to leave my team-mates for three months? This will be the one and only time I'll be out injured for an extended period like this during my career.

As usual, I take the news on the chin and process it, then do everything I can to come back as quickly as possible. The question arises as to where I'll go for treatment and what kind of treatment I should get. I talk to the boss, who advises me to go elsewhere. 'Coming to the training centre every day and seeing your friends on the pitch when you can barely walk is a big ask, mentally speaking,' he explains. I listen to him and go to do part of my rehab at the European Centre for Sports Rehabilitation in Saint Raphaël, in the south of France, where I'm looked after by a very competent team. As well as receiving superb medical care, I also have the opportunity to benefit from physical and mental training alongside a master in the field, Tiburce Darou, who sadly passed away in July 2015. A friend of Arsène Wenger, he worked with many top athletes to get them back on their feet after injury, including footballers Yoann Gourcuff and my friend Robert Pirès. He was renowned in the industry because he knew how to get the best out of each one of us, both physically and mentally. The boss knew this and I experienced it for myself.

At the end of these two weeks in France, I get home pumped up and determined to come back stronger than ever before. I continue my rehab at Colney before returning to competition on 22 November for a match against Manchester United.

Bursting with energy and raring to get out there, I finally step on to the pitch in the 77th minute against Manchester United when we're down 2-0. I pull one back 18 minutes later with a nice half-volley past David de Gea that lands in the top corner. We lose in the end, but for me the match represents a triumphant comeback.

On 16 September 2015, I start the European season in a Champions League match against Dinamo Zagreb. I get a yellow card for dissent, then I'm sent off just before half-time after a second yellow card for an avoidable foul. My team is down to ten men because of me, and we slump to a 2-1 defeat. I'm hounded by the English pundits and fans alike, who give me a ton of abuse and call for me to be replaced by my rival, striker Theo Walcott.

I put these troubles out of my mind, get my head sorted out and battle to get back in favour with the manager and fans. Three months later, I help my team get through to the last 16 with my first hat-trick for Arsenal, against Olympiakos. I become, after Thierry Henry, the second player in club history to have scored a hat-trick in the Champions League. The press, having shot me down in flames a few months earlier, are now praising me to the heavens and calling me 'the Greek god'. This turnaround doesn't bother me one way or the other. I'm well used to the changing moods of the press. It's all part of the game.

When I get back from Euro 2016, the boss summons me for a chat. I have a bad feeling about this. 'You've just played in a major international tournament and had the disappointment of losing in the final,' he says. 'It's normal to go through a phase where you need to unwind mentally as well as getting over the physical tiredness. I'm going to give you time to process everything.' I take on board what he says, but I press on as normal.

Over the course of various matches, however, I notice that Wenger is tending to go for a different type of striker from me. He's starting me less and less in favour of Alexis Sánchez, who is very effective up front. I don't write myself off, though, and just keep battling on to win back my place until the match against Crystal Palace on 1 January 2017 during which, with the now legendary 'scorpion kick', I score the goal that without a doubt will remain the most glorious of my career. It wins me the FIFA Puskás Award for the best goal of the year.

On 28 September 2017, during a Europa League match against Bate Borisov, a Belarusian team, I score my 100th goal across all competitions wearing the Arsenal jersey. I've only scored 16 this season, however, and the tide starts turning against me. In the summer of that year, the manager had signed a forward, Alexandre Lacazette, who he wants to play up front – in other words, in my position. I lose my status as first-choice striker and become number two. It's a hard blow, especially since the World Cup is fast approaching. I need to get a lot of game time to have any chance of being selected. The question arises over whether I should leave my club. Everton are aware of my situation and get in touch. I meet the chairman and the manager, Ronald Koeman, who express their keen interest in me. Their strategic plan is interesting.

I'm still hesitating, though. Throwing in the towel isn't what I do. My head's buzzing with questions. Should I not be fighting to win back my place on the team? If I stay here, do I risk missing out on a World Cup? I think back to the great times I've had at Arsenal. And then there's the fact that Arsène Wenger wants to keep me.

I'm not getting anywhere in my efforts to untangle all these conflicting thoughts, until something unexpected happens that helps sway my decision.

My mum calls me to tell me about Nicole, one of her friends who, like her, is a member of the evangelical church, and who has the gift of prophecy. 'Nicole has received a message for you,' she tells me. 'Shall I send it to you?' I say yes. Deep down, I'm not that surprised. I have prayed a lot over the past few days to try and find a way out of my dilemma, asking God to show me the way. Perhaps I'll get an answer to my questions. The prophecy tells of a cow in a field who is tempted to go and explore other fields, believing that the grass will be greener there. But the pasture where she grazes has nourished her for years.

The metaphor is an echo of my real-life situation. This club has allowed me to showcase my talents, to earn money, to flourish. I want to seek pastures new because I'm imagining that I'll find better elsewhere, but will the grass really be greener at Everton? The prophecy continues and orders me to listen to the voice of wisdom, to not want more, nor too much. Now is not the time to leave. I must put my trust in the Lord, who will guide me when the time is right. I remain silent for a few moments. I'm not going to leave Arsenal.

Two months later, Koeman is fired by Everton. How would my future have panned out there with a new manager? The next day, I go to see Arsène Wenger in his office, 'I've decided to stay at Arsenal. I'll compete for my place as long as I get a fair shot.' I've never regretted my decision.

Six months go by, however, and my situation gets worse with the arrival of striker Pierre-Emerick Aubameyang. Despite 105 goals and 41 assists in 254 games with Arsenal, my club stats over the past year and a half are dropping sharply: seven goals since the start of this season, 16 the previous season.

Didier Deschamps hints that I'm in danger of not being selected for the 2018 World Cup and encourages me to change clubs. I ask for a meeting with Wenger,

'I want to leave. I've got a World Cup to play in six months. I can't become third string, that's not a option.' With all the grace and humanity he's famous for, the manager replies, 'I understand. I'll never do anything to stand in your way if you want to seek new challenges. I know what you've brought to the club, I respect you and I'll do everything in my power to let you fulfil your potential elsewhere.'

It's January 2018, and we're right in the middle of the transfer window. My agent swings into action. Borussia Dortmund are interested in a loan, but the prospect of starting from scratch in another country, with everything that entails, is not very tempting. Jennifer agrees, especially as she's nine months pregnant. Roma and Sevilla also get in touch, but I don't follow those up any further. I want to stay in England to keep things stable for my family.

Through my friend Nordine, I hear that Chelsea manager Antonio Conte likes the look of me and is considering getting me in. Chelsea! This English club holds the joint record with Manchester City for lifting the most silverware in the last ten years. I'm flattered. I get hold of the manager's contact details and I approach him. His message is clear. I'll be up against a top striker, Álvaro Morata, but if I make a name for myself we'll be able to work well together. The only fly in the ointment is that there are rumours Conte doesn't get along with the directors. He has one year left of his contract with Chelsea. In these circumstances, will he extend it? I'd be taking the risk of ending up at a club with a new manager who isn't the one that signed me. It's no big deal, though. I accept the offer and my transfer is made official on 31 January 2018, in the final hours of the transfer window, for a fee of £18m. I leave Arsenal with the sense that I took the right decision at the right time.

I'll never forget that Arsène Wenger gave me the chance to pursue my dream of playing in the Premier League at Arsenal. A childhood dream which, through hard work and perseverance, I made come true. Those five and a half years with the Gunners let me take my career to the next level. More than that, though, I developed as a person. My real strength of character was formed during my time at Arsenal and continued to grow during the years I was there. Even more significantly, I became a father. And I mustn't forget my faith in Christ, always present in my life and giving me more courage and determination every day.

Like the previous clubs I played for, Arsenal was the logical next step in my career and in my life's journey. I had a respectful relationship with everyone who worked for them. I met some wonderful people there who made it so easy for me to settle in, and I will treasure my memories of Arsenal for ever. Whatever else was going on, I made sure I always behaved impeccably so that I'd leave everyone with a good impression of me. A few days after celebrating my 100th cap for France, I received a letter from Arsenal congratulating me on my great achievement. What class.

And so my time at the club ends with me having chalked up three Community Shield and three FA

Cup victories. I'm still grateful today for the affection and respect Arsenal fans show me if I bump into them anywhere. Their thoughtfulness touches me deeply and makes me proud to have been a Gunner and a member of the Arsenal family.

Chelsea

The first year at Chelsea goes well and I get to play in the World Cup in Russia. On 5 February, I play my first match with the Blues. Ten days later I score my first goal, against Hull City in an FA Cup fifth-round match. We get to the final and take home the cup after I score a beautiful goal in the semi-final, watched by both my brothers, who have come over for the occasion. 'A goal à la Messi,' according to the journalists.

I have amazing memories of this match. It takes place at Wembley – my special place and my lucky stadium. I've finished undefeated in every FA Cup match I've played there with Arsenal or Chelsea.

Lifting the trophy doesn't save Antonio Conte, however, as he's sacked on 12 July 2018, and replaced by Maurizio Sarri.

In August 2018 I return to my club after France's victory in the World Cup. I share playing time with Álvaro Morata. Six months later, the new manager lets my team-mate go and brings in Gonzalo Higuaín, his protégé from Naples. Another blow for me. I'm not an idiot. I know this player is going to be the manager's favourite.

My game time is dwindling, but I have enough mental strength to keep my place on the team and get the job done on the pitch. The manager has me playing mostly in Europa League matches. I net ten goals and then, on 29 May 2019, during the final against Arsenal, I score one, provide an assist and win a penalty. We win this prestigious competition against my old club, crushing them 4-1. I'm establishing myself on the European scene and finish top scorer in the Europa League with 11 goals in 14 games. This means I've set a new record for most goals scored by a French player in a single European season.

Unfortunately, my efforts and performance are not enough. On 4 July 2019, our new head coach Frank Lampard takes the reins. History is repeating itself. I have stiff competition from two forwards: Michy Batshuayi and the young Tammy Abraham, who was an EFL Player of the Month the previous season and finished the Championship's second-top scorer with his loan club, Aston Villa. The manager is going to make him first-choice striker, ahead of me. He plays brilliantly in every match. My game time is getting cut just as Euro 2020 is looming on the horizon. At this point, we have no idea that the championship will be delayed for a year because of Covid-19.

I'm in pretty much the same situation as I was in at Arsenal. Once again, I'm under pressure from Didier Deschamps, 'Olivier, I know what you bring to the French team, but if you don't get more time on the pitch, I'm not going to be able to call you up for the Euros.'

The season has barely started so I don't despair just yet. There are still a lot of matches to play. I'm starting out with the handicap of not being the first-choice striker. I'm not in the strongest of positions, but what I do have is motivation. I roll up my sleeves and start trying to win back my spot, to no avail. Right from the opening match of the Premier League season, I discover that Frank Lampard wants to play the 21-year-old Abraham up front. I find myself back in the number two spot, on the subs' bench again. We lose 4-0 to Manchester United.

The gaffer gives me my chance in the UEFA Super Cup. I have a good match and I manage to score, but we lose on penalties to Liverpool. I'm in the starting line-up again for the next match. Despite a strong performance, I'm taken off in the 60th minute and I don't start again until 30 November 2019. In the meantime, Abraham is on blistering form. He scores two doubles and a hat-trick in four matches. He's establishing himself once and for all as the first-choice striker. I'm barely getting any minutes at all now, the equivalent of a match and a half in four months. Chelsea are due to play away at Southampton in mid-October. The manager comes to see me, 'I'm only taking one back-up striker for the bench and it's going to be Michy.' It's a hammer blow.

In October 2019, I'm called up to play for France. Before I go and join Les Bleus I really want to make my position clear with Frank Lampard. Seeing how determined I am, he hints that when I get back from international duty things will all work out and he'll give me my chance. I trust him, but all the same I warn him that if my situation hasn't improved by January, I'll have to think about leaving. I can't settle for being relegated to third spot. I'm a competitor, I need to play and, most important of all, there's a hard task ahead with France in July 2020, probably the last competition of my international career. I don't want to miss it. What I really want is to be happy. And I'm not happy.

On the bench

After I get back from playing with France, I have a month to wait before I'm back on the pitch as a starter, in a match played on 30 November against West Ham. I'm there because Abraham is injured. Then nothing. December turns out to be complicated. The manager brings me into the squad but Batshuayi gets to play. I don't set foot on the pitch once. Instead, I'm left to wait it out on the bench. I feel powerless and have a horrible sense of being surplus to requirements.

I'm more annoyed at the situation than particularly affected by it. It's not that I'm losing any self-confidence. I know why I've been sidelined. My qualities as a striker are not in question and I know what I can do for my team. I'm simply on the receiving end of the decisions made by a manager who would rather play a young guy with a different set of skills. But I'm tired of being at the mercy of one person's decisions. I might have won a World Cup, but somehow I keep having to start all over again.

I'm stressed beyond belief. I'm scared I'm going to miss out on the Euros. And apart from anything else, I just want to play. It's like there's something missing, and I can feel its absence both physically and mentally. I'm missing out on competing and getting no chance to play at all. It's a horrible time. Come the weekend, I sit in my living room watching my team play on TV. And yet I continue to train, even when the team goes to play away matches.

I have to leave Chelsea urgently. When the transfer window opens, on 1 January 2020, I'm on the market. Clubs are aware of my situation and contact my agents. First up is Lyon. They make a firm and serious offer. I talk with the owner, Jean-Michel Aulas, and his advisor, Gérard Houllier, then with manager Rudi Garcia, who offers me a starting position. It's tempting. I turn him down, though: Lyon might be a major French team, but my preference is to seek a challenge outside France which will let me broaden my horizons and compete for another championship somewhere new. I'm lucky enough to have already won the league title in France with Montpellier. It's not just a question of money, although I do take that into account. When I'm choosing a club, I look first at its strategic plan and consider the quality of life my family would have. The salary comes after that.

The main reason behind my decision to reject the move is something else altogether, however. I mention it to the Lyon directors but ask them not to disclose what I've said to the press for fear of starting a whole controversy around it. I'm revealing it here just for the sake of honesty and transparency. The problem was that I couldn't see myself playing for Karim Benzema's boyhood club. There has always been a supposed feud between me and Karim who, at the risk of repeating myself, I have absolutely no problem with. But ever since 2015, when I was first named in the starting line-up for France, some fans have been divided. On the one side there are the pro-Girouds, on the other the pro-Benzemas, who still hold a massive grudge against me and blame me for Benzema's absence from the national squad.

I knew that if I signed for Lyon, I'd be taking a risk that my family and I could end up having a bit of a rough time of it. I didn't want to take that chance and for us suddenly to find ourselves in what I imagined could be quite a hostile environment.

Inter Milan: a bitter disappointment

Lyon are not the only club in the running. There are other French clubs interested in me, as are Inter Milan, who are especially keen. We start talks. Their strategic plan appeals to me a lot. They have the Italian championship title in their sights. I put pressure on my agent Michaël, who makes several trips over to Italy and negotiates my contract. Everything is going well on that front. He then goes to Chelsea to start talks with Marina Granovskaia, owner Roman Abramovich's right-hand woman.

My transfer fee is £6.5m, which is much lower than before: I'm 33 now and I only have six months left with Chelsea. Both parties are more or less in agreement on the financial terms when a problem arises; Chelsea agree to let me go on the condition that they can get a replacement for me. I'm not playing at all, yet Frank Lampard doesn't want to risk being left without a striker if a player is injured. I don't understand why it's only now that he's waking up to what's going on. He's known for several months that I'm going to leave.

Time is running out. It's 20 January and the transfer window closes at midnight on the 31st. I spend hours on the phone with Michaël. I'm hanging on for news 24/7. Everything is finalised with Inter, and all that remains is to find my replacement at Chelsea. In my head, I've already left England. The days go by, then a call from Italy scuppers my plans even more. Inter need to sell a player to Roma to make room for me. A problem was discovered during this player's medical and means his transfer can't be completed. My departure for Milan is thrown into doubt. My nerves are frazzled. I pray a lot.

A few days before the transfer window closes, the problem gets resolved and I begin to feel hopeful again. I'm certain I'm going to Milan. Jennifer and I are on standby, ready to move house as soon as we get the green light from my agent. We're starting to think about our children's schooling in Italy and where we're going to live. We're looking ahead to our new life. But just four days before the 31 January deadline, the sky falls in. I hear that Inter Milan also wanted to buy Christian Eriksen. The club had a budget to buy both of us but on 27 January, the director of football calls my agent and tells him they've spent their entire budget on Eriksen. They can't afford to bring me over too. I can't believe it. In the space of a few minutes, all my plans are wiped out. I have no future. The Euros, still scheduled for June 2020, are rapidly moving out of reach. I'm gutted.

I receive another prophecy from Nicole. She tells me that I mustn't cling on to my desire to leave. I'm done.

This emotional rollercoaster I've been on for the last month has left me completely worn out. My agent calls me. 'What are we doing? Are you going to risk staying at Chelsea or do you want to give yourself every chance of playing in the Euros?' Without any hesitation, I give him my answer, 'I have to leave.'

The clock is ticking

We have four days left to find a solution. Michaël gets back to work. Clubs know what's going on and start reaching out again. Arsenal's rivals Tottenham are ready to sign me. Aston Villa, too, and the Rome club Lazio, whose director of football comes to Chelsea to show me they're interested and try to convince Lampard to let me go. Even François-Henri Pinault, the businessman and owner of Rennes, calls me directly. 'I'm not used to doing things this way,' he tells me, 'but we have great plans and we'd love to bring you over.' The clubs are all standing by, watching

191

and waiting. My family and in-laws support me and I get calls from team-mates Benjamin Pavard, Laurent Koscielny, Mathieu Debuchy, Hugo Lloris and others, all of whom encourage me not to lose hope. I hang around Frank Lampard's office, pestering him every morning before training. I'm doing everything in my power to make things happen, but nothing is helping. Over and over again I get the same answer, 'If I find someone, you can go. Otherwise you're staying here.' I get the feeling he's just toying with my career. He's thinking only of the interests of the club. The longer things drag on, the more I suspect I'm not going to get the outcome I want. I go to training anyway. Always trying to do the right thing.

On the morning of 31 January, a few hours before the transfer window closes, my team is all set to go and play an away match. The manager breaks it to me that I'm not part of the squad. 'You're staying here,' he says. 'You never know, things might sort themselves out in the course of the day, and you'll have time to sign.' That afternoon, the hours race by. There's nothing new to report. It's over.

Believing again

I've really hit rock bottom. I'm absolutely on my knees, unable even to react. But my family manage to take my mind off things and I bounce back quickly enough. I don't let myself mope around or wallow in self-pity and I refuse to see my future as all doom and gloom. I come to terms with what has happened, pick myself up and move on. I have to turn things around, so I get myself into a positive mindset and start believing again. Whatever happens, the coming months are going to be exciting: playing as many matches as possible with Chelsea, meeting the targets set with my club, especially in the European Cup, and playing with France in the Euros.

I decide to trust Lampard. He assures me that he'll give me a chance in the coming weeks, and he promises to give me more opportunities. I believe him, especially since he has said as much to the press too. He has taken a public stand and honoured his commitments.

I return to the squad on 17 February, as a substitute against Manchester United. After two and a half months without playing, I'm overjoyed to step out on to the pitch again. I think about Jesus. I get off to a good start and I score in the 70th minute, although my goal is ruled out for being offside. Five days later, the manager starts me against Tottenham. I throw myself into the match and in the 15th minute, I fire home a low shot past my friend and France team-mate Hugo Lloris, who's in goal for the opposing team. It's the goal that clinches the match. I can't hide my delight. I'm back! A few minutes after the final whistle, Lampard comments in a post-match interview, 'Olivier Giroud played brilliantly and did a fantastic job for us. I know I can count on his professionalism and his skills. He was very good. He's obviously given me a lot to think about.'

I start in the Champions League again against Bayern Munich, a difficult match against a far superior

German team. I don't score, and we go down 3-0. Strangely, I keep the faith more than ever. The future proves me right. I start the next three league matches, despite Chelsea's number one striker Tammy Abraham returning from injury. I play a key role in two of them then score in the third, against Everton. It's a fresh start. Nothing can stop me. Nothing, that is, except the unforeseeable, the unthinkable.

The cataclysm

On 8 March, we don't imagine for a second that the match against Everton will be the last one we play for a long time.

A few weeks before, I'd heard something about a virus doing the rounds in Wuhan. At first, I don't pay much attention, I must admit. It's in China, thousands of miles away. But one detail catches my eye: governments are ordering the restriction of mass public gatherings in their countries. This includes football matches. Some sporting events have already taken place behind closed doors. I'm now starting to take things more seriously and I wonder if the end of the season will be disrupted. What do the next few months have in store?

The answers are not long in coming: the club doctor summons us to discuss the situation and brings us up to speed about new procedures we have to follow. We're no longer allowed to shake hands. Hand sanitiser will be made available. And he goes on. All the same, we continue training as normal – until 12 March, that is, when we learn that Mikel Arteta, the Arsenal manager, has tested positive for Covid-19, then immediately after that so does Callum Hudson-Odoi, one of my Chelsea team-mates. That brings everything to a halt. The whole squad has to quarantine for 14 days. We're asked to return home and self-isolate there. Otherwise, life continues as normal in England.

I join my wife and children at home. I'm not imagining that this lockdown will last much more than a couple of weeks. Then events start gathering pace.

Boris Johnson decides to join other European countries in asking all citizens to stay at home. Businesses close their doors, as do restaurants, bars and schools. Life comes to a standstill. Football too.

Jennifer and I explain to the children what's going on. Jade, the eldest, understands; the two little ones, not so much. We're glued to the news on TV with its rolling updates. The news reports are alarming. The virus is spreading. I think of my relatives, some of whom are over 60 and at greater risk. I'm worried about them, although I know they're being careful.

Oddly enough, I'm not afraid for myself even though I've been in direct contact with a player who was carrying the virus and was therefore contagious. I'm young and healthy, so I'm convinced nothing can happen to me. I'm in regular phone contact with my friends. Some have been affected, including Blaise Matuidi who never even realised he had contracted the virus. At no point do I isolate myself from my family. I continue to kiss my kids and sleep in the same bed as my wife.

The days go by and the prospect of going back to work becomes ever less likely. The club thinks ahead: it has an exercise bike delivered to each of us then sends us a fitness programme to do at home – resistance training using whatever we have to hand, a strength workout for the lower body and running for cardio. It's essential that we keep in shape, so I go for a run in the park near my house every other day. The government allows us to do this, provided we take all necessary precautions. Twice a week, a video call is set up for the whole team. We're happy to meet virtually to follow the instructions of the fitness trainer who gets us working our abs and core.

I need to get some fresh air and burn off some energy. I'm not used to being cooped up indoors all the time. On the suggestion of my friend Lars, who has been given the job of planning outings, I agree to discover the joys of cycling. Against all expectations, I discover a taste for this activity. I cycle around 40 miles in one day with my friends Robert Pirès, tennis player

Jérémy Chardy, Jens Clausen and Romain Rousset. It's physically challenging and I push myself to my limits, but I get a lot of enjoyment out of turning the pedals. These outings are quite literally a breath of fresh air. I get my revenge on my friends, who are better cyclists than me, when we go jogging in the park. I'm in such good shape thanks to the club's fitness programme that they struggle to keep up with me.

I manage to do about ten hours of sport a week. My body is not in any pain, but my mind is certainly suffering. I miss football, the competition, the adrenaline of matches, my friends and the team. I train alone. I don't touch a ball or lace up my football boots for two months. This has never happened to me before and I have to admit it's tough. I realise that my life as a footballer is key to my mental stability.

Lockdown isn't all bad, though: I can take an active part in family life, something I'm not used to. I find I have the time to look after my children, to cook with them. I watch them go about their lives. It's rewarding to be with them. With them in lockdown too, it's difficult to keep them occupied 24 hours a day, so we allow ourselves a little outing into the private garden of our apartment block once a day. We all play together, just us, without coming into contact with anyone else.

These extraordinary times have increased my awareness of the world around me: an awareness of environmental issues, which makes me want to get more involved in this cause. Like most people, I've seen nature reasserting itself and pollution decreasing dramatically. This virus, so brutal for humanity, has given our planet a few months of respite. On the one hand death, on the other rebirth. I realise that we should take what's happening to us not as a punishment, but as a warning. A warning to stop for a moment, look around and take better care of everything that surrounds us. To focus on family and friends.

This event has shown us just how fragile – and therefore precious – life is. It's now up to us to learn from it. We must learn to keep things in perspective and enjoy the here and now when we're lucky enough to be in good health. What I write seems obvious, of course, but when we're caught up in the whirlwind of our daily lives we tend to forget what's most important. Ultimately, this virus has given us some much-needed breathing space and time to reflect.

Will there be a before and after? I don't know, but I hope so.

Chelsea: the story continued

Circumstances stopped me from playing football, temporarily calling time on my career – and my future too. Before lockdown, I was hoping to turn things around so that I could stay at Chelsea. I battled to get an opportunity to play again and for once I succeeded. Frank Lampard kept his promise to give me a chance, and I was able to take that chance and prove that I deserved the confidence he had in me. By late March 2020, the question of moving on is no longer on the table. My agent contacts the club to ask what they have in mind for me. The directors have no hesitation in expressing their desire to keep me there. My contract is renewed for a year, with an option to extend it by a further 12 months, and made official on 20 May. I'm pleased and reassured by this. My adventures with Chelsea aren't over yet.

At the beginning of May 2020, our manager sets up a remote meeting to see how we're getting on and find out if we feel ready to come back. I'm ready. We resume training on 18 May, in groups of five, with no small matches or mini-tournaments. It's not until the beginning of June that life really gets back to normal, from a footballing perspective anyway, and even then there are a few minor changes. Every morning when we wake up, we're required to take our temperature, then answer yes or no to a series of questions that get sent to our phones: do we have a cough, any aches and pains, difficulty breathing, a sore throat? Before we enter the stadium for training, our temperature gets taken again. In addition, Premier League players have to take a PCR test for Covid every three days. This is a requirement before we're allowed to play.

Despite the situation, I'm just happy to finally be back on the pitch. On 21 June, Father's Day, we play our first game since lockdown, against Aston Villa. I score a goal, which I dedicate to George Floyd, the man who died after being restrained by police officers in the USA, and to the Black Lives Matter movement.

My six goals in seven starts prove decisive as the season draws to a close. No one would have put any money on me playing for the team again after these last few chaotic weeks, never mind me scoring eight times in the ten games I've played since the transfer to Italy came to nothing. This resurrection, as we might call it, I owe to Frank Lampard who stayed true to his word and gave me a fair shot. I've also played a big part in helping the team secure our top-four spot, thereby qualifying for the Champions League. Despite losing in the FA Cup Final to my old team Arsenal, I'm getting the feeling that my return to favour is making next season look very promising indeed.

Training starts again on 22 August, after three short weeks of well-earned holiday time. The club has spent a lot of money during the summer transfer window. Among other new signings, Hakim Ziyech, Timo Werner and Kaï Havertz have been brought in to strengthen our forward line. The competition promises to be tougher than ever and I'm beginning to fear the situation is going to change again, and in a way that is not to my advantage. My doubts are confirmed when we start our bid for the Premier League. I kick off this season on the bench because the manager prefers to play Werner up front. But I hang on in there and continue my efforts to move back up the pecking order.

A period of grace

Meanwhile, a happy event takes place: the birth of my baby daughter Aria. A wonderful gift from heaven. She is due at the end of November, but it seems increasingly unlikely that she is going to stay put until then as Jen is already experiencing mild contractions quite regularly, so we decide on a planned delivery, scheduled for 18 November. I get a call-up to play for France the day before and I pray that nothing will happen until after I get back.

I'm nervous, but I still manage to have a good match against Sweden and return to London the next morning to find that my daughter has waited for me. We pack a bag and head to the hospital. I join Jen in the delivery room and am there for the birth. At around 8pm our little cherub comes into the world, and I feel just as emotional as I did when my other three children were born. I stay with my wife and our baby, then go home to take care of Jade, Aaron and Evan. Early the next morning I'm back at the hospital. I wouldn't dream of missing the chance to give Aria her first bottle and enjoy my first skin-to-skin with her. Late that afternoon, the three of us go home.

And life as a footballer continues. I come on as a late substitute in a Champions League game against French team Rennes, scoring the last-minute winner with a fierce header. On 24 November the manager announces he'll be starting me against Sevilla the following week.

The day of that match, 2 December 2020, will remain one of the happiest of my whole career. It will be only the third time so far this season that I've been in the starting line-up.

Off we go to Seville where we find everyone enjoying an Indian summer. There is a really nice vibe in the city. The team is feeling pretty relaxed. We have breakfast on the hotel terrace and the day passes peacefully. By the time we're ready for kick-off, the heat is subsiding. I have a good feeling as I start warming up for the match ahead.

I score a fine goal with my left foot after a superb passage of link-up play, and we're 1-0 up at half-time. The match is wide open as the teams are both through to the knockout stage and are only playing to decide who wins the group. Fed by a good pass from Mateo

Kovacic, I bear down on goal and chip the ball over the keeper with my right foot; 2-0. Then, in the 74th minute, my fellow Frenchman N'Golo Kanté delivers a perfect cross from the right which I finish off with a flicked header in front of the defender; 3-0. I've netted a perfect hat-trick this evening: left foot, right foot and header, just like I'd done in the Europa League match in Kiev the previous season. But I haven't finished yet. Eleven minutes later, as I jump for another cross in the penalty area, the defender shoves me in the back. The ref gives me a penalty and I decide to take it myself. I'm still out of breath from the previous bit of play, but I tell myself that it's not every day I get the chance to score a quadruple, especially not in the Champions League.

I hold my nerve and score my fourth goal of the evening, joining the elite group of just 14 other players who have scored four or more goals in a single Champions League match. I feel a huge sense of pride and I can't help but look heavenwards, thanking God for this unforgettable gift.

My team-mates shower me with congratulations once we're back in the dressing room. They expect me to say a few words, and so I do. As always, I stress the teamwork aspect, and I thank the other players whose hard work gave me the chance to shine tonight. And, as is traditional, I get to keep the ball from the match, which the whole team signs.

My performance has earned me a starting spot for the next game, against Leeds. I score once again and I'm enjoying this period of grace. I'm getting picked to start match after match, and in eight starts, I've scored nine goals in all competitions since the beginning of the season.

New man at the top

I don't know it at this point, but on 16 January 2021 I'll play my last match with Frank Lampard at the helm. We win 1-0 at Fulham but I take a hard knock to my ankle and I'm out for the next two games.

Rumours that our manager is leaving have started to do the rounds. We're aware that he's had his head on the block for some time now. We stay focused on our work but we're obviously affected by what's going on. We're in a state of limbo. Finally, the inevitable happens and on 25 January, Lampard is sacked. At this point we're ninth in the Premier League, six points behind the team in the all-important fourth spot.

I'm keen to talk to the manager before he leaves so that I can thank him for the last 18 months, which have seen us play in a cup final – even if we didn't win – and a UEFA Super Cup Final. I'll remember him as someone who is absolutely passionate about football and a true man of his word. I must admit that things haven't always been easy, particularly when he first arrived and favoured Tammy Abraham over me.

It was at that point I realised I would have to fight to secure my spot on the team. I rose to the challenge and played a lot of matches, but never regularly enough.

The fact is, I never really felt at ease during the whole Lampard era.

Nevertheless, I'm grateful to him for keeping the promise he made in January 2020 that he would give me the opportunity to get back on track. I took it with both hands, rounding off what was an outstanding season by qualifying for the Champions League and finishing with a top-four spot. This experience allowed me to show both manager and fans that I would always step up to the plate and be ready to fight for my team, and that I'd be able to turn a bad situation around whenever necessary.

I'm pretty happy when the new coach arrives. Thomas Tuchel brings with him fresh ideas and solid credentials, particularly the string of titles Paris Saint-Germain have won with him in charge. Our team needs someone to breathe new life into it, and I think he might be just the man we need to give us a shot in the arm as we're currently struggling in the race for the Champions League. The Tuchel effect clearly works, as five and a half months later we'll be holding that prestigious trophy aloft.

The man who arrives at Chelsea is happy, enthusiastic and quietly confident. Very quickly he summons us for our first meeting, telling us how glad he is to join our team. 'It's a nice Christmas present,' he says.

Tuchel impresses me with his spontaneity and good humour. He immediately brings a certain dynamic and a breath of fresh air to the club. The day before the first home match, against Wolverhampton, he comes over to have a word with me. 'I see you as an important player in this squad,' he tells me, 'and I'm relying on your experience.' Reassuring words which at that point bode well and suggest a bright future ahead.

Unfortunately, the reality turns out to be different. To begin with I get a regular starting slot, then it's one match yes, one match no. This continues until the end of February when I score that memorable goal – an overhead bicycle-kick – against Atlético Madrid.

Two weeks later, during the traditional team talk before the match, I learn that I'm going to be sitting it out on the bench. I'm surprised, although I don't let it stop me from staying focused on the game. The next day, the manager explains that he made a tactical decision to use faster strikers in order to play in behind. I'd have thought I'd be a good fit since, as he said himself, we needed to pass the ball out wide and hit crosses to destabilise the defence. It won't surprise anyone to know that getting on the end of crosses is one of the things I do best. So I'm thinking at this point that if I'm not brought on for a match like this, then what hope is there for the future?

I feel a bit desperate when I realise I'm becoming nothing more than a back-up plan. My minutes are getting drastically cut and I haven't started a match since an FA Cup fixture in mid-March, three and a half months ago. It's a hugely worrying time for me. I'm feeling pretty down about it all, but at the same time I know I don't have much of an argument, as our team is moving up the table regardless and we're fully engaged in Champions League ties. Step by step, we're getting closer to victory, first seeing off Porto, then heavyweights Real Madrid in the semi-final, before beating Manchester City in the final. I have conflicting emotions. I'm flipping between joy and anger, and all the while feeling a grievous sense of injustice that I've been sidelined when I'm actually the team's top scorer in the Champions League with six goals to my name.

My thoughts turn to the national team and the Euros that are fast approaching, put back by 12 months because of Covid-19, and I'm preparing for the worst. Didier Deschamps is concerned for me. He lets me know that this lack of minutes has massively compromised my chances of making it to the championships. He's not telling me anything I don't already know. I can see the situation for what it is and I know that my role with Les Bleus is going to be different this time. I'm not afraid of being dropped from the squad altogether, but it's inevitable that I'm going to lose my starting spot. At this point, there is nothing to suggest that Karim Benzema is about to be brought back into the fold.

Goodbye Chelsea

I'm definitely going to have to leave Chelsea if I want to give myself any chance of continuing my career at the highest level. This is it. I'm determined to leave this time, and I ask my agent Michaël to seriously consider any offers that come in. Whatever happens, I will not be playing for Chelsea next season, I'm convinced of it. I'm strengthened in my conviction the day we leave for the Champions League Final. I'm feeling sad and already a little nostalgic. The following day marks the end of the season and the team are about to go their separate ways. My heart clenches. The manager makes a speech, after which I go up to him and say, 'Thanks for everything. We've achieved amazing things together. Although it's been difficult for me sometimes, please know that I've learned a lot from you.' I can tell from the way he looks at me that he understands I can't carry on like this. We say goodbye for what we both know is the final time.

I have very fond memories of Chelsea. In the three and a half years I was there, we won the FA Cup and the Champions League. I hope I'm remembered just as fondly, both as a player and as a person. I'd like to think so, as I received many nice messages afterwards.

Various clubs are now starting to reach out, including AC Milan. Jennifer and I discuss the situation at length. For a while now she has been preparing herself for my leaving Chelsea. For personal reasons to do with our family's wellbeing, she would like to stay in England and is secretly hoping that I find a club in London if at all possible. But the idea of moving on and signing for AC Milan is starting to seem like a foregone conclusion as far as I'm concerned. My heart has belonged to the great Italian club since I was a child. AC Milan have been home to my favourite player Shevchenko, as well as Papin, van Basten and all the other legends.

My transfer takes its own time, with long weeks of negotiations between my agent and the club. In June, Michaël organises a FaceTime meeting with Paolo Maldini – another AC Milan legend and now the club's technical director – his sidekick Federico Massara and myself. The Italians are keen to show that they're interested and I need to feel like they really want me. The same goes for coach Stefano Pioli, who I have a long chat with. We talk about Zlatan Ibrahimovic, who recently made a major comeback, signing for AC Milan for a second time after a spell playing for MLS club LA Galaxy in the States. His successful comeback that unfortunately ended in injury at the close of the season. Zlatan is 40 now and probably won't be able to play every match, which is one of the reasons the directors want to bring in another experienced player to join what is a very young team. They make no promises and don't say anything about what my role would be in the team. Would I be first or second choice? It will be up to me to prove myself and earn my spot.

I emerge from these discussions reassured and feeling that they're really keen to welcome me to the club. I've been completely won over.

Conquering Milan

A few days later all parties reach agreement so on 16 July, while on a family holiday in Grenoble, I put pen to paper and sign my contract. I'm absolutely delighted. I know I've made the right choice. This club represents an amazing opportunity to take on a fresh challenge and give my career a boost.

During a press conference after I arrived in Italy, journalists questioned me about the fact that I'd actually been about to sign for rival team Inter Milan. I didn't deny it, but told them that I am a Christian and the fact that I was sitting there before them showed what God had had in mind for me. It's true that I almost ended up playing for Inter, but I held off and finally signed for AC Milan. It was always going to happen that way. It was my destiny and that's all there is to it.

I've received many kind messages and been given a very warm welcome, especially from Italian supporters, some of whom I had the chance to meet outside Milanello, AC Milan's training centre. So far the adjustment period has gone smoothly. I've settled in well and I feel comfortable playing in Italian football for the first time. I proved this when I scored with my very first touch of the ball in my first match, a friendly against Nice, after just four minutes of play. Two weeks later, I scored a double against Panathinaikos.

Milan will probably be my last big European club. My motivation and my desire to win titles remain as strong as ever, though. I'm not hanging up my boots just yet.

Euro 2020: down to earth with a bump

I'd have liked to start this section in the same way as I did Chapter 1, when I described the World Cup Final on 15 July 2018, using the same words, the same fervour, the same emotions.

I wish I could write again about our gang of mates, and how happy we were, how united and invincible we felt. In other words, I'd have liked to describe a completely different experience from the one that Euro 2020 actually turned out to be.

Our defeat will probably not leave us unscathed, but we have to accept it and learn from it if we are to bounce back and move on, just as we did when we lost to Portugal in the Euro 2016 final.

I know many people will be eagerly awaiting this part of my story, hopeful that I'm going to provide a tell-all account of why France got knocked out so early and what was really going on behind the scenes in the team. Some people will be expecting me to reveal here all the secrets that weren't talked or written about in the media at the time.

At the risk of causing disappointment, even if there was any behind-the-scenes gossip to share, I wouldn't be doing so here. I refuse to give our critics any more ammunition or to feed their fantasies. I'm not afraid of controversy, but I don't want to stir things up and talk about what really went on during the Euros for one simple reason: this story is not only mine to tell. It concerns the whole squad, players and staff alike. And so I'm only going to discuss a few points here. These involve me and me alone, and are nothing more than my own personal feelings about the events of June 2021.

The match against Switzerland in the last 16 was ours to win and we blew it. We were leading 3-1, then Switzerland managed to score with nine minutes remaining and make it 3-3 in stoppage time. The final penalty of the shoot-out, taken by Kylian Mbappé, was saved by Swiss goalkeeper Yann Sommer, and just like that we were out of the tournament.

We should have won, and in all honesty I admit we were already thinking ahead to the next match, to be played against the winner of Croatia v Spain. Each of us had already talked about which of the two teams we'd prefer to play in the next round. Who could have imagined that things would turn out this way? We hadn't lost the desire to win and we were as motivated as ever. The manager had victory in his sights, of course, the worst-case scenario being that we'd get knocked out in the semis. We're still trying to work out why things went so wrong for us. If we had won against Switzerland we wouldn't still be discussing the match now.

One thing is certain: we were not as strong nor as solid as we'd been in previous years. Our collective strength had weakened. Why was that?

Didier Deschamps did his duty as head coach and took full responsibility for the situation. It wasn't that mistakes were made, he said, but rather that he had made strategic and tactical choices that did not work out. It's an honourable admission to make on his part and says a lot about the man he is, but it's not that simple. Other factors came into play that I would describe as 'aggravating circumstances'.

As had been the case in previous championships, the FFF, with our comfort in mind, had chosen base camps suitable for our needs. There were no complaints as far as that was concerned, but the issue was that we could have been living in the most comfortable place in the world and we would still have felt the urge to escape from time to time in order to let off a bit of steam, just as we'd done during the 2018 World Cup in Russia. To have the chance to put football out of our minds for once, to talk about something else and simply enjoy a nice meal out as friends rather than team-mates, are rare opportunities that are vital for the life of the group.

However, because of the ongoing pandemic, we were cut off from the rest of the world. To avoid any risk of contamination, we had to adhere to a strict protocol that had been put in place and isolate ourselves in a sanitary bubble from the very start of training. No more evenings out, no more opportunities to decompress, no more meeting and greeting fans. For the first time, we stayed holed up in our hotel. We started to feel increasingly suffocated and this inevitably had an impact on the atmosphere within the squad. What affected us more than anything else, however, was the ban on seeing our families, although a few of us broke that rule. When we play in international tournaments, our wives and children breathe new life into us. We need to be able to hug them and kiss them. They give us renewed energy, help us keep a sense of perspective and give us the strength to face the pressure head on. Why were other teams granted this privilege and not us? This state of affairs, added to our defeat, explains the tension that fans unfortunately had to witness erupting on the pitch as well as in the stands.

The return of Karim Benzema

It's also worth mentioning the return of Karim Benzema to the national side. Some people believe he might unintentionally have knocked the squad off kilter. The manager maintains that this is not true. I'm not going to comment on what anyone else thinks, as the only opinion I can reasonably give here is my own.

I must say that Didier Deschamps was never anything less than honest with me in the months leading up to Euro 2020. In view of what was going on with Chelsea and the fact that my playing time had been so drastically cut, he made it clear that my role in the national team would be different, in other words that I no longer had a guaranteed starting slot. I was in no position to argue given that I was barely playing at all for my club. Deschamps made no promises and I joined the squad with full knowledge of the facts.

However, what I didn't know was that Karim had been recalled. I learned about it at the same time as the public did, when the manager announced the names on the list. The news hardly came as a massive surprise – what with rumours flying around and leaks to the press everyone had pretty much grasped that the Real Madrid striker was on his way back. But at that precise moment, I said to myself, 'If Karim comes back, you are toast. He'll be number one whether he scores or not.' I wasn't mistaken. Karim quite unwittingly left his team-mates in the shade and ousted me for good. That didn't particularly shock me, because the excessive media fanfare surrounding his return could have been predicted, but it must be said that the press did not display a huge amount of sensitivity in pushing Antoine Griezmann, Kylian Mbappé and the rest into the background and only talking about Karim, which in turn put additional pressure on him. Footballers all have an ego, all the more so if they're strikers. The manager tried several times to calm the media down but the story had gathered its own momentum.

Questions flooded through my head one after another. Why did the manager call Karim up when only a few months ago his return to the squad wasn't even remotely on the cards? The answer seemed obvious to me, although once again, it's only my personal opinion. He recalled Karim because the squad needed him. Let me explain. Our qualifying matches for the World Cup were tough going and, let's face it, the attacking line were not exactly on blazing form. I didn't start any of the three matches at the finals. Deschamps knew I wouldn't be bringing my A-game due to my lack of playing time at Chelsea and so he wasn't really going to be able to rely on me once we got to the championship itself. By recalling Karim, he wanted reassurance and to be able to give the team a fresh impetus.

I then wondered about the timing of it all. Why had the manager brought Karim back so late when he hadn't played with the national side for five years? Kylian, who joined the French squad in 2017, had never played a single match with Karim. How would we be able to find our bearings and click as a team in so little time? The first three matches proved to be a struggle for him and it wasn't until the game against Portugal that he finally broke free and scored a double.

Finally, I wondered if things were actually going to gel at all after Karim had been away for five years. How was he going to fit back into a squad with such a strong showing in recent years as European runners-up and world champions? He took a risky gamble, but it must be said that he rose to the challenge. We welcomed him back into the team and, for his part, he made every effort to fit in. It wasn't that he upset the equilibrium of the squad just by being there. It was more that by being there he created a tactical imbalance in our game. It wasn't his fault, but it was painfully obvious. We lost our collective strength. That sudden imbalance was what damaged the team.

Karim and I hadn't seen each other properly since 8 October 2015, when he had played his last match for France. Our paths crossed again during the first leg of the Champions League semi-final in 2021, when Chelsea played Real Madrid. After the final whistle, we greeted each other before we went into the dressing rooms. We gave each other a high-five and I congratulated him on his goal. It was a brief but cordial reunion.

We next met at Clairefontaine when the squad got together for the Euros. The ongoing Covid situation meant that the layout of the restaurant had changed. The large table where we used to have lunch and dinner together had been replaced by several small tables to allow social distancing. Karim sat next to Raphaël Varane, whom he knew from Real Madrid. With them were Lucas Hernandez, Benjamin Pavard, Antoine Griezmann, Léo Dubois – and me. We were chatting away about this and that in what was a good-natured, friendly atmosphere. I was watching Karim, thinking to myself that he looked like he'd never been away. I focused on the good of the team and put my pride to one side to make him feel comfortable and part of the squad. It wasn't a huge effort to do so.

Kylian and me

Before I end this chapter, I want to revisit the controversy I unwittingly caused. It happens after a friendly against Bulgaria that France win 3-0. Karim takes a nasty blow to the thigh and is forced to come off. I replace him and score in the 83rd and 90th minutes. I'm elated because once again I've been able to show that I'm there when the team needs me. After the match, a journalist, meaning no offence, calls out, 'So after a very quiet start you managed to score?' The way the question was worded undoubtedly annoyed me, but nevertheless I reply, 'I was a little quiet because sometimes I make runs and the balls just don't arrive. I'm not saying that I always make the best runs, but I try hard to provide solutions in the box. With two good balls from Ben [Pavard] and Wissam [Ben Yedder], I was able to finish well, but we could have scored more goals if we'd been more efficient.' Then I go on to say, 'Personally, I'm very happy to have been able to help the team. You say that I wasn't seen much at the start, but maybe we could have found each other better.' Note that I said 'we could have found each other' and not 'he could have found me'. The journalist comes back with, 'We can sense a note of bitterness in your words,' to which I reply, 'There's no bitterness, don't worry.' That's the sum total of the exchange that affected Kylian so badly.

Why did my words cause such an uproar? At what point did I condemn Kylian? Why did he feel so got at? I admit that I didn't understand his reaction nor that of some journalists who persist in saying that I was blatantly referring to him.

I'm going to clear things up once and for all. I've never used the media as a mouthpiece to address any of my team-mates. When I have something to say I will say it to the other person's face. In any case, I wasn't going to risk starting some sort of controversy a few days before the Euros. So, I wasn't aiming a barb at Kylian. That being said, as soon as I knew I'd upset him, I had to try and sort things out. First, I sent him what I'd said, and then that evening I went to his room to explain what I'd meant. He did seem hurt and criticised me for speaking to the media instead of directly to him. I reiterated what I said, showing him that I hadn't pointed the finger at him personally. We talked about it but I am not going to go into exactly what was said here.

The next day, everything seemed to be back to normal. We played on the same side in a training match and we managed to find each other perfectly well. I had already drawn a line under the whole story. It took him a few more days to forget about it.

Epilogue

That's all I have to say about the events of June 2021, a month we would all like to forget. We were knocked out of the Euros when we were favourites to win and had, I quote, 'the best attacking side in the world'.

Can I really say that the outcome was unfair? No. The Swiss team snatched victory from us and they deserved to. As for us, we have to admit that we did not exactly excel at any point during the tournament. Top-level sportspeople like us are used to these ups and downs. We know that a match can change course dramatically at any point and that having been on top of the world since 15 July 2018, we were bound to come crashing down at some point. It is what it is.

The match ends and we're devastated. How the mighty have fallen. Kylian wanders around the pitch, wild-eyed and distraught. I can tell right away that he's blaming himself. Other team-mates are in tears. Tensions erupt between players and between members of their families. Didier Deschamps tries to calm us all down and then invites us to follow him towards the stands to meet the fans. We then go back to the dressing room in what is a deafening silence. Didier follows close behind us. His sadness and disappointment are etched on his face. He's silent for a moment, then puts his manager's head on. His first words are, 'I take responsibility for this defeat.' Then he asks us to hold our heads high and to stand united and stick together as we always have. He keeps his speech brief. Now is not the time to settle scores, nor to try to find any possible explanations for what has happened.

The atmosphere is almost too oppressive to bear until Kylian stands up and apologises to all of us for missing the penalty. Each of us says a few words to reassure him, reminding him that all the greatest players have been there too. We go back to the hotel without saying a word, then get together with Hugo Lloris, Ben Pavard, Antoine Griezmann, Léo Dubois, Lucas Hernandez and Clément Lenglet. We spend hours picking the match apart over and over again before everyone finally goes back to their own room. It is a very long night.

The next day, we land at Le Bourget airport, say goodbye to each other then go our separate ways. I experience a powerful emotion at this point, a sadness similar to how I felt the day I left my Chelsea team-mates, knowing that I wouldn't be coming back.

Thursday, 26 August 2021: I turn on the TV and learn that I have not been selected for the upcoming World Cup qualifiers. The tournament is 14 months away and nothing is certain about what my future holds with the French national team.

8

The National Team

ONE-NIL, TWO-NIL, three-nil.

It's 12 July 1998. I'm 11 years old, and it's St Olivier's Day, my feast day. I'm at my cousin's house in Cavaillon watching the World Cup Final, France v Brazil. My face is painted in the colours of the French flag and I'm bouncing up and down on the sofa with excitement. I get to my feet, shouting abuse at the players as if they can hear me. I'm shaking with nerves every time Brazil look like they're stepping up the pace even a fraction. They could come from behind at any moment. I admire Zinedine Zidane's genius and his efficiency in front of goal, Youri Djorkaeff's technique, but also the work Didier Deschamps puts in. He's a more technically understated player, his presence on the pitch more low-key. But I notice his charisma. You really have to know football to appreciate what an important position he plays in the team. It's a thankless role, sometimes, with the player sacrificing himself for the others. Deschamps doesn't shine – he allows his team-mates to shine. He does an impressive amount of work in the background.

It's a few minutes before the final whistle. I still don't feel I can relax. Then Emmanuel Petit seals it by scoring the third goal. My cousin and I jump into each other's arms, roaring with delight, and launch into the French national anthem, singing at the tops of our lungs. Off we go into town to join the crowd, who are all going crazy. We chant Zidane's name. His face is projected on to the Arc de Triomphe in Paris. He's the hero of this final. The hero, full stop.

A few days before that, maybe during the semi-final, my friends, twins Johann and Damien Almodovar, had reminded me that when I was little I'd told them

I'd be world champion one day. Like all kids who are passionate about football, I dreamt of being the next Zidane or Robert Pirès and lifting the World Cup. And yet I played for a long, long time with no specific aim in mind other than just kicking the ball around with my friends. It was only around the age of 16 or 17 that I began to consider a possible career in football.

Clairefontaine

When I'm 14, an unexpected opportunity presents itself. I win the Interdistrict Cup, which brings together teams from the Rhône, Savoie, Ardèche and Isère regions of France. I'm in the Isère team. After that, the best players from the wider Rhône-Alpes area – including me and my friend Alexis Lafon – are selected to play in the National Cup, a French championship of sorts. This is to be held in Clairefontaine, the training centre for the French national team. The inner sanctum of the French football elite.

I walk through the gates for the first time. It's a feast for the eyes. Several football pitches, each with immaculately mown grass, take up the entire left-hand side. A little further on, I see a sign that says 'Press Room'. I imagine this must be where the players and manager do their interviews. At the far end of the vast grounds stands the famous château that is home to the French team when they get together for international duty. We're not allowed in, but I admire it from a distance and I begin to dream. My coach calls me to attention, rousing me from my thoughts. It's time to get training.

During the various matches, scouts from the FFF and professional clubs, youth team coaches, and agents are all watching from the stands. We win the National Cup. I score two goals in the final and finish top scorer of the tournament. A few days later, the FFF informs my club – Grenoble Foot 38 – that I've been selected to take part in a training camp at Clairefontaine during the next school holidays. Hugo

Lloris, Yoann Gourcuff and Yohan Cabaye are going to be there too. After this training camp, I return to Grenoble and life goes on.

The next time I set eyes on Clairefontaine is when I've been selected to play for France for the first time.

First steps with Les Bleus

The manager of France at this point is Laurent Blanc. Part of the World Cup-winning team of 1998, he has been appointed as an urgent replacement for Raymond Domenech after the 2010 World Cup in South Africa, where – as every French person well recalls – the players went on strike. Laurent has a colossal task ahead of him: drawing up a new strategic plan, reconnecting with the public and restoring the team's image, currently in tatters. This new era marks the return of Philippe Mexès, Karim Benzema and Samir Nasri. Players like Adil Rami and Yohan Cabaye are called up for the first time. The goal is simple: qualify for Euro 2012.

The 2010 season brings mixed fortunes. By the end of the following year, however, Les Bleus have won 15 matches in a row and qualified. In November 2011, they begin their preparations for the Euros with friendlies against Belgium and USA at the Stade de France.

I'm 25 years old and starting my second season at Montpellier. I'm fighting fit and playing at the top of my game. A few indiscreet whispers tell me that Laurent is thinking about asking me to join the national team. He started his career at Montpellier and still has a few friends there who drop hints that I'm going to be called up. I don't get any such call. I learn that I've been selected when the list of players is announced on TV. It's such an immense accolade. My childhood dream: the biggest, the best, the most beautiful – and the least expected.

So it's November 2011 and here I am back in Clairefontaine. This time, the taxi drops me off outside the château. I'm impressed. A giant replica of the World Cup trophy takes centre stage on the lawn, marking France's 1998 victory. The memories come flooding back.

I'm greeted by Laurent, who takes me under his wing. He is calm, reserved, level-headed. He and his assistant Jean-Louis Gasset form an ideal partnership, complementing each other perfectly, the latter leading training sessions and regularly playing the role of ringmaster on the pitch when a change of focus is needed.

In 2012, when internal problems that I don't wish to dwell on here reared their ugly head within our team, I realised that Laurent was not the type of man to bang his fist on the table. Not because he lacked authority, but because he wanted everyone in the squad to take responsibility for themselves. He was far too nice sometimes. Some of the young players at the time thought they had spotted a weakness in the way he did things and were taking advantage of it.

At any rate, from the minute I first arrived at the château, I found him to be a very normal, very nice guy.

After the introductions, Guillaume Bigot, France's videographer who captures on film the players' initial reactions when they arrive, offers to show me to my room and give me a tour of all the facilities. Then it's time for lunch. There are no allocated seats, but players nearly always sit in the same place. I look for an empty chair and sit down next to Bacary Sagna, whom I've never met before.

I'm quite certain that if I'm really going to fit in here, the onus is going to be on me to approach people. I'm pretty sociable and I like to chat and swap stories. I get on fine during this first meal. The managers play close attention to how well we settle in and become part of the squad. My team-mates are making it easy for me. There are a few I already know and get on well with, like Mathieu Debuchy, who will later become godfather to my son Evan, plus Yohan Cabaye, Laurent Koscielny and Hugo Lloris.

I remember in particular Patrice Évra, who was nicknamed 'Uncle Pat' because he was one of the oldest players. Patrice had a bad reputation that he was struggling to shake off. He had been captain of the 2010 French team and, as such, was seen as the standard-bearer for the strike in Knysna. When I got to know him, I discovered he was a really sound guy, generous and full of integrity. He's one of the players who really helped me settle in.

When I became an 'elder' of the French team myself, I made sure I welcomed the new arrivals in the same way. Florian Thauvin, for example. He's only 24 years old when he comes here for the first time and he seems intimidated by the place. I know him a little; we've played against each other before. I greet him, 'Congratulations on being selected. Welcome!' I know from having been in his shoes that these words are comforting to hear.

I don't have the luxury of indulging my emotions, as real life intervenes. On 11 November, I come on in the 55th minute against the USA in the Stade de France. The fans are quiet, with just a few chants audible from the stands. The crowd's anger and resentment after the events in Knysna are still palpable. Few people come to support us at Euro 2012 in Poland and Ukraine. We've lost their trust. Only winning matches and behaving impeccably both on and off the pitch will enable us to make our peace with the French people.

I play my first two matches as a substitute, coming on for Karim Benzema. On 29 February 2012 I start as striker instead of him and score my first goal for France in a friendly against Germany. In May 2012 I join the list of players selected to take part in the Euros, again as a back-up for Benzema, who doesn't score at all in the tournament. After that, I clock up one selection after another. I'm still the number two striker, though, and as a result of that, I don't get a lot of game time.

Didier Deschamps

It's June 2012. Laurent Blanc steps down as the boss of the national team. His track record as manager is largely good as far as the game itself is concerned, but the process of patching things up between Les Bleus and the public has not even begun. We're still carrying around the legacy of Knysna. Didier Deschamps takes over as manager, and in his very first press conference, he makes his position crystal clear. As far as he's concerned, it's an honour to wear the national jersey and represent our country, and this matters above all else. He extols the virtues of togetherness and team spirit, but also the individual mindset of each player. The message gets hammered home. 'There is no room for error,' he says. 'If I feel that any player might be endangering these values, it will be my job to take action.'

The tone has been set.

The manager has an aura and an air of legitimacy about him that result from his past career and achievements, a track record we all can only dream of equalling. His charisma and natural authority mean he never has to raise his voice when he speaks to us at crucial moments. He is a great communicator, with an impressive persuasiveness. With simple, well-chosen words, he instils in us the cult of winning, and makes it quite clear that we're all important – all 23 of us, and not just the 11 on the pitch. Each of us has a role to play in our quest for victory.

More than anything, though, I appreciate his human side. He makes every effort to get to know the man behind the player. He gives us advice without ever forcing his opinion on us, unpicking every situation in a bid to find the best solution. If ever a player has a problem, he summons him for a one-to-one chat in the drawing room of the château, where there are never many people around. This is what he did with me when I wasn't getting enough game time, first at Arsenal and then at Chelsea, to have a hope of competing in international tournaments. He never interferes in our personal lives, unless he feels that something is negatively impacting our work, for example if he's concerned our lifestyle isn't as healthy as it could be. But, again, all he does is tell us what he thinks, nothing more, 'I'm giving you my opinion, but you do what you want with it.'

For him, it's always a question of give and take. He puts his trust in us and we repay that trust on the pitch. When he starts me in the round of 16 match against Nigeria in the 2014 World Cup he is sending me a strong message, a sign of his confidence in me. He has high hopes for me, and I have to live up to them. We've been doing this since 2012. I know by now what he expects from me and he knows what contribution I make to the team. Over the years, we've got to know each other and we can talk quite openly. I can tell just by the look in his eye when he's not happy, but he'll never put a player down if he falters or makes an error during a match, just as he won't shower him with praise in the opposite kind of situation.

He inspires respect. We never call him 'Didier', but 'manager' – like we do all managers. We use *vous*, the formal French word for 'you', when we talk to him; he uses *tu*, the familiar form of the word, with us. We are very respectful of the hierarchy, although that doesn't stop us from pulling his leg if he slips on the pitch or fluffs a centre pass in training sessions. He has a good sense of humour and really likes to wind us up. We know that if we make a loose touch or a bad pass, we'll never hear the end of it.

From a human and a footballing standpoint alike, Didier is the most important manager I've had in my career. He has put his trust in me and given me great opportunities.

Right from his first day as manager, we understand that things are going to change. 'There is nothing more important than the national team,' he keeps reminding us. We represent our country, we are privileged to be part of the squad and every day we must be aware of the responsibility that falls on our shoulders. We are to wear the blue jersey with pride. Our behaviour must be exemplary, and that starts with 'La Marseillaise', the French national anthem. Everyone, without exception, must sing it. He also insists on how we should behave towards our fans: with respect and humility. Finally, we must show professionalism and put the interests of the squad before ourselves.

Armed with these instructions, we set out to recapture the hearts of the French people and start winning matches again.

France–Ukraine

Wednesday, 15 November 2013. France meet Ukraine in a 2014 World Cup qualifying play-off tie. We lose 2-0. In the dressing room, which now resembles a wasteland, a deathly silence reigns. Didier rouses us, 'We have to keep believing.' This defeat seriously compromises our chances of playing in the World Cup and puts our manager's job on the line. We need to win the second leg, but also pull off the feat of qualifying for a World Cup with a three-goal margin. No team has ever managed to achieve this.

It's difficult, but not impossible.

Back at Clairefontaine, the manager gathers us round after dinner. 'Well, that was a slap in the face,' he says. Then he talks about solidarity, hope, pride, the battle, the team. In ten minutes, everything has been said. Disappointment gives way to a burning desire to win. We can do it. We WILL do it. Operation Commando is launched. We prepare ourselves mentally, praying that the French people will put their resentment aside and cheer us on. We need to feel that the country is behind us. A few hours before the game, we leave for the traditional pre-match walkabout. Fifty-odd supporters are waiting for us outside the hotel.

On the evening of 19 November, we welcome Ukraine to the Stade de France. I'm on the subs' bench, but I don't mind – it's the team that counts, and the fact that we absolutely have to come back from the brink and qualify. When the bus arrives, we're surprised by the size of the crowd flocking into the stadium. We ain't seen nothing yet. As we come out of the dressing room, the manager says, 'Come on, guys, let's give them hell out there!' We emerge from the tunnel to find a jam-packed stadium. The FFF has put a French flag on every seat, and they're all fluttering in the wind. The supporters are going wild. Even before kick-off, they're cheering us on, chanting our names, singing in unison. It's impressive. More than impressive. The French are on side.

Right from kick-off, we exhibit the mindset of warriors. We win just about every one-on-one, we create multiple chances, we're threatening and dangerous. Mamadou Sakho scores the first goal. We don't get too excited. There's still a lot to do. Focus. Twelve minutes later, Karim Benzema drives it home with a second goal. We're now level with Ukraine. At half-time, the manager has just one comment: 'We're nearly there, just keep doing what you're doing.'

In the 72nd minute, it's defender Sakho once again. Just like Lilian Thuram, who wrote his way into the history books with a brace that put us through to the

1998 World Cup Final from 1-0 down, Sakho nets the third, the winning goal that qualifies us for the 2014 finals in Brazil. The crowd are on their feet, completely delirious. It's a freezing cold evening in Paris, but no one is even thinking of leaving the stadium. We are in perfect harmony with our fans. Overcome with a sudden burst of national pride, I politely take the announcer's microphone off him and launch into 'La Marseillaise'. The crowd joins in. The atmosphere in the stadium is electric. It's a moment of incredible communion and emotion.

The manager has tears in his eyes. 'You've made history,' he tells us. 'Bravo! Stepping up to the plate like that is just as much about mental strength and the desire to do it as anything else. You've got both of those in spades. Now, go and enjoy the moment!'

This match remains one of the most vivid memories of my career. We savour the whole experience from start to finish. But our schedule means we quickly have to get our heads down and find our focus again.

Karim Benzema

Karim starts and I'm a sub. I continue my progression in the team by trying to get as many minutes as possible. I've made it my mission to play to the absolute best of my ability with the aim of planting a seed of doubt in the manager's head and therefore getting an opportunity to play. Basically, I'm in a competition against my team-mate.

The manager starts me in a 2014 World Cup qualifying group game against Georgia, in March 2013, and I score. In October 2013 I score twice against Australia, and in May 2014 I score another brace against Norway. Karim is having a goal drought and not managing to score at all. Didier has waited a long time before making this decision because, like all of us, he considers Karim to be a top-class player. He finally gives me my chance and I grab it. I score France's 100th goal in the World Cup finals, against Switzerland in the group stage in Brazil.

Karim and I played for France together for three and a half years and had a completely normal relationship during that time. He isn't a close friend of mine, not like Hugo Lloris, Laurent Koscielny or Mathieu Debuchy. I'm not a close friend of his either. But we've never as much as had cross words with each other, despite being rivals since late 2013. We often get together in the sauna after Monday training and have a perfectly civil chat.

Karim has no reason at all to have any kind of grudge against me. By 2014, he is without a doubt the number one forward. In 2011, when I tiptoe in, he's already well established in his position. Newcomers to the French team who could potentially be rivals for his spot – such as André-Pierre Gignac, Bafétimbi Gomis and Kevin Gameiro – have never managed to put him on the bench. He's not remotely worried about losing his starting place. There is not a single player who scares him, and that includes me. He only starts to feel threatened when he stops scoring, and at this point he has gone 1,222 minutes and counting without a goal. The manager puts me in the starting line-up more often. I represent a bigger threat and am seen as an alternative striker for the national team, especially as I'm having a good season with Arsenal.

Of course I aspire to be number one, of course I want to play in more matches, of course I want the manager to give me opportunities. I make no apology for that and I'm not ashamed to say it. Does that make me an imposter? It's fair enough that a competitor would want to play, isn't it?

My relationship with Karim doesn't change. The press, on the other hand, pit us against each other and have a field day with the whole situation, fuelling a controversy that they created in the first place. The journalists make us out to be enemies, which we're not. They try to get me to admit that I want to take Karim's place. I am very cautious about what I say and I choose every word carefully. I don't want to come across as pretentious or cocky. Nonetheless, I agree to requests for interviews because I'm proud to wear the jersey and happy to speak on behalf of the French team.

In December 2015, a scandal erupts. Mathieu Valbuena has reportedly been approached by blackmailers who have allegedly tried to extort money from him for a compromising video, in what will become known as the 'sex tape scandal'. Karim is under investigation on suspicion of being an accomplice in the blackmail. He will not be called up to the French team so logic dictates that I'll take his place in the starting line-up. The controversy grows arms and legs. Fans take sides, and everything is reported in the press.

The issue rears its ugly head at every possible opportunity. Didier Deschamps knows he's going to have to justify Karim's absence during every press conference. The problem I'm having with lack of game time inevitably raises the question of Karim's return to the squad and whether the manager will keep me on after that. If I finish a match without scoring, the question of whether I really deserve to be there gets raised again, no matter how useful I've been to the team. It's exhausting.

I don't beat myself up about it. A player gets dropped and another player takes his place; it's all part and parcel of being a footballer.

With the Euro 2016 kick-off just weeks away, I'm having a hellish time of it. I've become a scapegoat, a punchbag for French fans to have a go at. In May 2016, during a friendly against Cameroon in Nantes, I get dog's abuse from one section of the crowd. A minority, admittedly, but a very vocal minority. That morning, I'd seen a kid standing outside our hotel holding up a banner that read 'Giroud, please get injured'. I get that the coming match is going to be difficult, but I naively convince myself that if I get the job done on the pitch, I'll manage to appease the supporters. I have absolutely no clue what I'm going to have to put up with.

The boos start echoing round the stadium from the first moment I touch the ball. It's annoying, but I don't let it throw me off balance. I give it all I've got on the pitch and I'm careful not to make the slightest error. I

2018 World Cup

Above and below: With my daughter, Jade. © DR

Above: The photo with the flag was not taken on the night of the World Cup Final, but during Euro 2016, after the victory over Iceland (5-2) in the quarter-finals at the Stade de France. © Matthias Hangst/Getty Images/AFP

Below: 16 July 2018, Élysée Palace. © Xavier Laine/Getty Images

2018 World Cup

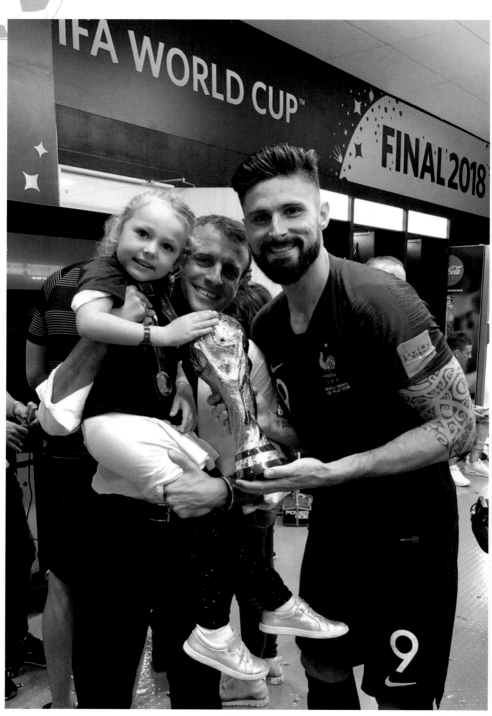

With President Macron and Jade, in the locker room, after the victory in the World Cup. © DR

Top: With Jen at Istra base camp.© DR

Bottom, left: With Aaron, 4 June 2019, the day of the presentation of the Legion of Honour. © DR

Bottom right: With the presidential couple on the day of the presentation of the Legion of Honour. © DR

Chelsea

Above: Celebrating my 'Messi' style goal in the FA Cup semi-final against Southampton (2018).

© Dan Istitene/Getty Images/AFP

Bottom and right: The evening of the Europa League Final, won in Baku against Arsenal (2019). © Shaun Botterill/Getty Images/AFP

With Jen and our three children on the pitch at Stamford Bridge Stadium (2019). © DR

UEFA Champions League Final victory against Manchester City, 29 May (2021) © Alamy

29 August 2021, with Stefano Pioli, head coach of AC Milan, celebrating the 4-1 victory over Cagliari Calcio (2021). © Nicolò Campo/LightRocket via Getty Images

score in the 41st minute. Nothing works. The booing starts again, louder than ever. I find it hurtful the way the French public has fallen out of love with me, and I see it as a massive injustice. The following day, the headlines in the press read 'Giroud, the unloved'. My team-mates rip me to shreds singing 'The Unloved', a song by the famous French singer Claude François. I force myself to laugh.

Later, with hindsight, I chose to interpret the fans' hostility as fear. Fear that we weren't playing competitively enough. Fear that we might not win. Fear that I was going to be the reason for our defeat, that we would fail because of me.

Until Euro 2020, Karim and I hadn't seen each other in any meaningful way since October 2015. Neither of us had tried to get in touch with the other. I respect him for the man and the player he is. He plays for a team that has won the Champions League four times. His skills are undeniable. I have no problem recognising his talent. But as everyone knows, if you're pursuing a career as an elite athlete, talent isn't the only thing you need to reach the top.

European Championship Final

This is a game I've already touched on briefly. There's no need to relive it all again. Everything has been said about why we lost against Portugal. Were we too confident? The answer is no. For some players, it was the first time in their careers they'd played in the final of a major international tournament. Had we already played our final against Germany in the previous match? It's not that either, even though we were pretty wiped after that match. We still had five days to recover, after all. Did Cristiano Ronaldo's injury make us think the European Championship was in the bag? Probably. Maybe we were subconsciously thinking that because the best and most dangerous player on that team was out of action, it would be easier for us to win. What I mostly think, though, is that it actually gave the Portuguese team a boost. Far from crumbling under the pressure, they regrouped and got the upper hand. This match is the worst memory of my career.

Victory is ours to take. We're playing in front of a home crowd. We create chances right up to the last second, when the ball, on a shot from André-Pierre Gignac, hits the post. And then we lose. At the final whistle, I sink to the ground. I'm in tears. Absolutely overwhelmed. It's all over. We've missed the opportunity to be European champions. What I don't imagine at this point, of course, is that two years later we'll be world champions. We're all just sitting on the pitch, my team-mates in tears too.

Thinking back on it, I believe that defeat helped us win the World Cup. We didn't want to have the same nightmare a second time. Paul Pogba said as much in the dressing room a few minutes before the final against Croatia, 'This time, we bring it home. No way are we going through 2016 all over again.'

Following the Euro 2016 final, in earlier anticipation of our victory the FFF has organised a party in a luxury hotel in an upmarket area of Paris. A party is the last thing we feel like, but we go anyway. Our families and friends join us. It's hot. There's an outdoor swimming pool in the middle of the hotel. No one goes near it. No one wants to. A lavish buffet is set up. A sympathetic DJ stands behind his decks, waiting to be given the green light to start. He'll make do with putting on a bit of background music. We have a quiet dinner, then go to bed, stunned by our defeat.

My life in blue

Over time the French team has become a second family. I've shared moments of intense joy with them, but we've gone through some tough times as well. I've found my place in the group. I'm one of the senior members now. The old guard. As I said before, I've formed close relationships with team-mates from the same generation: Hugo Lloris, Laurent Koscielny, Mathieu Debuchy. I also have a lot in common with some of the young players who came up later: Lucas Hernandez, Florian Thauvin and Benjamin Pavard. And then there are Paul Pogba, Antoine Griezmann, Blaise Matuidi and Raphaël Varane – we've shared unforgettable highs and lows from playing together. That inevitably brings people closer together. I'm on friendly terms with the rest of the team. The important thing is not to make enemies. And I don't have any.

I enjoy quite a special relationship with goalkeeping coach Franck Raviot. It's one based on humour. I find he has a unique way of expressing himself. He uses formal language that he embellishes with fancy words. He makes me laugh like a drain sometimes. Franck never takes offence and has no problem at all giving as good as he gets. I also have great affection for Raphaël, the team's head waiter, Nico Piry, the Nike representative, and Jean-Yves, our osteopath. Down-to-earth, genuine people. And, of course, not forgetting Guy Stéphan, the assistant coach.

Getting together at Clairefontaine is always exciting. Between training, meals, physio sessions and our evenings, we spend three-quarters of our time together. The only exception is at night, since we sleep in single rooms.

I'm very sociable, but sometimes I just need my own company, so I shut myself away in my room. I always take the Bible with me and read a few verses before going to sleep. Outside I can hear the younger players, who go to bed much later.

We have every evening off, but of course we're not allowed to leave Clairefontaine. After dinner, we play table football, cards or ping pong. The staff hang around longer to discuss upcoming matches or just put the world to rights. Occasionally, when we have four days off between matches, the manager agrees to let us go out from noon to 8pm. We go into Paris. For reasons that everyone will understand, it's difficult for us to just walk around town. We choose a quiet place for lunch, like the restaurant of a big hotel. Then we too put the world to rights.

Each of us likes to unwind in our own way. As soon as I take my seat on the bus ready to go to the stadium, I get out my phone. I start by reading Bible verses. Then I listen to music while I play Scrabble. I've become addicted to this game, that I used to think was only for people of our grandmothers' generation! What a great discovery. I also like chess. My chess partner is N'Golo Kanté. One day, when a journalist asked him about it, he replied, 'I play chess and I thrash Olivier Giroud.' When I came across the article, I asked him, 'How can you say that?' He replied, 'The guy trapped me into saying it.' I shot back, 'Okay, some day I'll tell the world that I crush you at Scrabble.' And now I have. Out of the 150 games we played in a year, he only beat me five times. On the other hand, I have to admit that the chess fan is better than me. The competition just never stops! We're too old to change.

We're not particularly superstitious, but we do have our rituals. For me, it's prayer. Before each match, I have a little chat with Jesus. I'm not the only one who does this. The first time Clément Lenglet played for France, I saw him a few minutes before the match started, sitting on a chair, eyes closed, hands clasped, with a rosary between his fingers. I went up to tell him about my own faith and to applaud him for praying openly.

Others, like Antoine Griezmann, like to let off steam by listening to music. Kylian Mbappé, Florian Thauvin, Thomas Lemar and N'Golo Kanté practise keepy-uppies. Blaise Matuidi, Corentin Tolisso and Hugo Lloris like to do a sequence of stretches. I do too sometimes. Everyone has their own thing. The colour of our shoes, contrary to popular belief, isn't anything to do with superstition. It's the kit manufacturers who make that decision.

Our strength lies in the fact that we have very different personalities. Some players, such as Griezmann, Pogba, Hernandez and Presnel Kimpembe, are pretty demonstrative characters and like to take centre stage. Blaise Matuidi, Steve Mandanda and Raphaël Varane are the spokesmen for the team. As our captain, Hugo Lloris, the most serious-minded of us, is often called on for comment. During the last World Cup, Pogba took on the role of leader, showing a side of himself that the public were unaware of. I'm more reserved, but I do sometimes say a few words before an important match. It's a way for me to release the tension and I motivate myself by motivating my team-mates. Finally, there are the quiet ones, like Kanté and Mbappé. The latter prefers to let his legs and feet do the talking. He's an introverted guy, focused and impressively mature for his age. He's as humble as he is talented.

As soon as we arrive at the stadium, we enter a 'bubble'. We have to do this so that we can get our heads down and concentrate on what's ahead. There are strict rules that have to be respected. Phone calls, for example, are banned from the minute we enter the dressing room. No more contact is allowed with the outside world. Everyone listens to their own music separately. Griezmann and Pogba will occasionally start singing and dancing just to lighten the mood. In 2018, they were joined by another livewire, Benjamin Pavard.

To warm up our muscles, we get a massage from the physio or osteopath. While we take this opportunity to relax, we give each other tactical or technical advice about the match ahead of us. And then, for some unknown reason, in the midst of this slightly tense atmosphere someone will crack a joke about a bad shot one of us made or a ball someone sent flying into the stands during the practice session. Whatever tournament we're playing in, the atmosphere in the squad is healthy and good-natured. We're a group of buddies, really.

In November 2020, I celebrated nine years playing for France. Competition is still in my blood. Every match is an intensely emotional experience for me, whatever the result. Every title I win, everything I achieve at club level, it all makes me very happy indeed. But, as the manager says, 'There is nothing that can equal the national team.' Playing for our clubs, we represent just the one city. With Les Bleus, we have 67 million French people supporting us.

I am proud to represent my country and I already know how much I'm going to miss playing for the French team, once it's all over.

9

Afterwards

Looking ahead

As long as my body keeps going and clubs are interested in me, I will play football. I want to live out my passion for as long as I can. But I do know that one day everything's going to stop and I'm mentally preparing myself for that day.

I'm afraid of what comes next. What does the future hold for me? What will become of me? How am I going to be able to deal with this major life change? Will my body be able to stand the abrupt end to daily physical training? The only thing I know for sure is that I will miss football terribly. The competition, the adrenaline rush when I score, the excitement before a match, the atmosphere in the dressing room, getting together with the team, my mates – everything that has filled my life for so long.

I often mention it to my friend Robert Pirès, who has already been there. He hadn't looked ahead to the end of his career at all. When he did hang up his boots, he enjoyed a few well-deserved days of rest. Then he got depressed. It took him several long months to bounce back. He warned me, 'It's now you need to start thinking about things. While you're in the spotlight and still playing. Once it's all over, you'll find your phone won't be ringing so much. So, look ahead.'

Look ahead, now that I can do. I'm good at thinking beyond the here and now, and I'm organised. I try to leave nothing to chance, so that I have as much control as possible over what happens to me. I know from experience that life is full of surprises and things happen that we can do nothing about but, probably because I'm an anxious type of person, forward planning gives me a focus and reassures me. I follow Robert's advice to the letter.

More than anything, I want to stay in the industry. I've been playing football since I could walk. I belong in this environment and I can't imagine changing direction now. Football is my life. But faced with this inevitability, what will I do? Who can I turn to?

A career change

Every now and again my agent and I discuss my post-football career. One day, he calls me and offers to introduce me to a coach who specialises in retraining footballers. He tells me, 'Go and meet with him. I'm sure he'll be able to help you.' A few weeks later, I make an appointment with Stéphane Ehrhart, himself a former footballer, who started an association called Afterfoot. It's aptly named. The aim is to help players optimise their careers and prepare themselves as well as they can for what comes next. Stéphane carries out an audit of my current situation in terms of sport, family, finances and assets. He gets me to complete some tests to gain a better overall picture of my personality, my talents outside football, my communication skills and so on, then he puts together a retraining plan for me.

For the past three years, we've been meeting face to face or remotely and together we're preparing for my future. I'll be staying in the football industry. I don't see myself as a manager, but rather as a director of football at club level. The broadcasting or film world will not feature in my future plans, I can safely say. I think these are jobs in their own right, too far removed from anything I'm familiar with. That said, I recognise that some former sportsmen and women have enjoyed a great deal of success in this area. I wouldn't say no if I got invited to take part in a TV programme once in a while or give my opinion sometimes, but that's it.

We're not at that point yet. I hope to remain a footballer for a few more years. Still, I'm being realistic here. At 34, my career is largely behind me. Perhaps now is a good time to take stock.

I could never have imagined that football would allow me to experience the emotions it has. I never thought I'd reach these heights. I've achieved one ambition after another. Most of them were hard-won. But I've always had this unwavering determination to move up the ladder and overcome all the obstacles in my way.

When I signed my first professional contract, my goal was to play in Ligue 1. Once I was in Ligue 1, I wanted to play in the English Premier League. My rise to the top wasn't complete until I'd been selected to play for France. Once I'd done that, I then made it as a starter and won the World Cup.

As soon as I achieve one goal, I set myself another. I'm always looking further ahead, moving from one dream to the next. So far they've all come true.

Some people think I have good karma. I don't really know what that means. I believe a good person has good karma, and that's what I try my best to be every day. But success doesn't come from karma alone. Talent isn't enough either – there are many different factors that come into play. Family and close friends play an essential role in the life of a top-level athlete and contribute hugely to their success. I am fortunate to have been born into a close-knit family who raised me with strong values that gave me a solid foundation in life. Jennifer has built a protective and caring bubble around me, which has allowed me to do my job with complete peace of mind.

My career wouldn't be what it is without my wife and kids. My family keep me in line and give me the boundaries and stability I need. When the demands on me become too intrusive, my family call me out and I make a bigger effort to be there for them. My life is rigidly scheduled, timed to the minute almost, especially where the children are concerned. Sometimes Jennifer and I have a little chuckle when we try to remember the last time we had the opportunity to just relax and watch a movie in our living room. It's not a common occurrence, that's for sure. Pretty much the only time I get the chance to sit down and relax is when I watch a football match on TV.

My day-to-day life is nothing special. I go to bed early, around 11pm, sometimes before that if I have a match the next day. I don't smoke and I rarely drink, only when I have friends round or on special occasions. Right from the very start of my career, my brother Romain, who is a dietitian, has kept a close eye on how healthy my lifestyle is.

I remember when I was living alone in Istres for the first time, he'd turn up at my house, open the cupboards and the fridge, and put to one side any food that he deemed unhealthy, too heavy or too fatty. It was thanks to him that I learned to eat well. I also know how to treat myself, mind you. I like the finer things in life – good wine and nice food. Now and again, I let myself go off the straight and narrow a little bit, like going for a McDonald's with my children every couple of months. A chef comes to the house four evenings a week and prepares balanced and varied menus based around vegetables, carbs and protein. The whole family benefits from this.

This strong family unit gives me the strength and the confidence that I lacked when I was starting out in my career. Romain helped me a lot there as well. He told me over and over again that I had what it takes to be successful. All I had to do was, and I quote, 'take your foot off the brake and just go for it'. I listened to him, and everything I've achieved has let me develop a strong sense of self-belief over the years. You absolutely need that, there's no doubt about it.

Didier Deschamps sometimes uses the word 'overconfident' when he talks about me. Maybe this is the image I project, the armour I wear in public, but I don't agree with him. I have experienced – and I still do – periods of doubt where I've had to do some soul-searching. I think I'm pretty good at listening to what people are telling me and taking criticism. However, at the start of my career, when I was playing for Istres and

Tours, I must admit I had an unfortunate tendency to rest on my laurels. I was the starting striker and sometimes I was a bit prone to not putting the work in and just assuming my place on the team was a done deal. My manager at the time, Frédéric Arpinon – someone who really meant a lot to me – never missed an opportunity to have a go at me whenever he felt I was getting a bit too settled in my comfort zone.

While I'm on the subject, there's another story I remember. When I was playing at Istres, my kit sponsors asked me to wear brightly coloured shoes. One day in the dressing room during half-time, Frédéric plonked himself in front of me and said, 'What are these shoes about? Do you think you're a movie star?' This remark followed me around for a long time.

Talent is not enough

As soon as I arrived at Montpellier, I realised I had no time to waste. I was already 24 and nothing was going to get handed to me on a plate. I stepped things up a gear, career-wise, through a lot of hard work.

The pressure and competition are so intense today at both club and national level that I can't afford to become complacent. I have to battle to earn my place on the team and then to keep it. The setbacks I've had have helped me become more mature. You don't get to be world champion overnight. Every player needs time to improve their skills and climb the ladder one rung at a time.

To be successful as a footballer also means accepting you're going to have to make sacrifices: missing out on a part of your teenage life, living away from family and friends, not always being able to share life's big moments with loved ones. On another level, I make sacrifices on the pitch for the good of the team. Like any self-respecting striker, I play to score. Sometimes, though, when I'm a few metres away from the opposing team's goal, I don't shoot but instead I pass the ball to a better-placed team-mate. The words of the manager are engraved on our minds, 'The group comes before all else.' This altruism is part of my personality and part of my game. I'm described as a 'target man' – a player who can get possession of the ball thanks to his stature and the way he plays with his back to goal. I'm a focal point for my team-mates and I like to hold the ball up or play flick-ons when the game prompts me to do so. My role mostly consists of finishing moves and scoring goals. I'm also a link-up player: I link with my fellow players to get them in the best possible position. My assist to my former Arsenal colleague Jack Wilshere with a one-touch pass is the perfect example of this.

This atypical attacking profile is less spectacular than that of Kylian Mbappé, who bears down on goal thanks to his super-fast sprinting and the way he dribbles the ball past opposing defenders, leaving them bewildered. We're both attackers, but with different qualities.

I've also learned over the years to get my hands dirty by running from one end of the pitch to the other or plugging gaps. That's what Antoine Griezmann and I did in the last World Cup, especially in the match against Belgium, where we stepped out of our usual roles to defend like midfielders. The goal remains the same: to win, even if the beauty of the game suffers as a result. Only a few football experts could really appreciate these efforts. The rest were content with writing that I hadn't scored once during the tournament.

Talent is not enough. Good fortune has an important role to play in a career as a footballer. The good fortune to be in the right place at the right time. The good fortune not to be hampered by injury. Crossing paths with the right people who will put their trust in us, who will believe in us enough to offer us opportunities and who will guide us all the way to the top.

I consider myself blessed for the choices I've made and the people I've met. It's thanks to them that I am where I am. I have only one regret: not scoring in the World Cup. But I wouldn't swap places for anything in the world. Finish as the tournament's top scorer or win the title? It's a no-brainer.

No, talent is not enough. There are rough diamonds out there, 14 and 15 years old, who will never become Ronaldo, Messi or Zidane, because they might have the football skills of a genius but they lack the essentials: discipline, hard work and perseverance. You have to work tirelessly. You have to hang in there. Never get discouraged by a jeering crowd or a manager's decision. Keep going. Remain humble and respectful. Learn from your failures and come back even stronger. We are competitors. The will to win must never leave us. We need our heads just as much as we need our feet. Mental strength is paramount. It has allowed me to overcome setbacks and bounce back after I'd been written off as finished.

My unwavering faith in Jesus, day after day, minute after minute, accompanies me in everything I do and makes me strong, because I have faith in life, in God, in myself and in destiny.

This is my story. The story of a kid from Froges, passionate about football, who made his wildest dreams come true through believing in them.

Career highlights

Club

June 2006: first three-year pro contract at
Grenoble Foot 38

2006–2007: first pro season at Grenoble Foot 38

2007–2008: Istres FC (14 goals in 33 games)

2008–2010: Tours FC (Ligue 2)

18 September 2009: scored four goals on Ligue 2's
Matchday 7 against AC Arles-Avignon

2010–2012: Montpellier Hérault Sport Club

8 August 2010: first Ligue 1 match, against Bordeaux

15 October 2011: scored first hat-trick in a Ligue 1
match, against Dijon FCO

26 November 2011: scored a hat-trick against FC
Sochaux-Montbéliard

2012–2018: Arsenal FC

9 December 2015: first hat-trick in the Champions
League at Olympiakos with Arsenal

15 May 2015: hat-trick against Aston Villa

1 January 2017: scorpion-kick goal against Crystal Palace (winning the FIFA Puskás Award for the 'most beautiful' goal of the year)

7 January 2017: captained Arsenal for the first time in an FA Cup match

28 September 2017: 100th goal in all competitions for Arsenal in Europa League match against FC BATE Borisov

January 2018: left Arsenal with 105 goals in 253 games in all competitions over five and a half years

January 2018: joined Chelsea FC

5 February 2018: first match for Chelsea

International

2011: Called up by Laurent Blanc

11 November 2011: first international match, against USA

29 February 2012: first start in the absence of Karim Benzema and first international goal in a friendly against Germany

2018 World Cup qualifiers: joined France's top ten goalscorers of all time, with 23 goals

2021: second top scorer for France (46 goals) behind Thierry Henry (51 goals)

Trophies and awards

2021: Champions League winner (Chelsea)
2020/2021: FA Cup finalist (Chelsea)
2019: Europa League winner (Chelsea); top scorer in the Europa League (11 goals); League Cup finalist (Chelsea); UEFA Super Cup finalist (Chelsea)
2018: World Cup winner (France); FA Cup winner (Chelsea)
2017: FIFA Puskás Award
2016: Premier League runner-up (Arsenal); European Championship finalist (France); Euro 2016 Bronze Boot (third top scorer of the tournament)
2014, 2015, 2017: FA Cup winner (Arsenal); Community Shield winner (Arsenal)
2012: Ligue 1 winner (Montpellier); league's top scorer (21 goals)
2011: League Cup finalist (Montpellier)
2010: top scorer and best player in L2 (Tours)

Acknowledgements

FROM THE bottom of my heart, thank you to all my family.

Thank you, Papi Henri and Mamie Yvonne. It's because of you that I have such unforgettable memories of our family Christmases and our holidays in Val-d'Isère with Matthieu.

Thank you, Papi Jean, for making me understand that you have to work hard in life to get anywhere. I will never forget your smile.

Thank you, Mamie Tonia, for all the special moments we spent together. I loved listening to tales of your childhood and the story of your life with Papi. The values of hard work, respect and humility that are part of who I am today are also down to you.

Thank you, Dad, for all the sacrifices you made. Because of you, we never wanted for anything. You are the best father anyone could wish for.

Thank you, my beloved Mum, for your unconditional love, your hugs and your tender words. You allowed me to discover the Christian faith that we are lucky enough to share as a family.

To Bert, Rom and Bé. You've looked after me since I was little, you've given me so much love and affection and each of you, in your own way, has been a role model for me.

Jen, I know you sacrificed your career so that I could live out my passion. But more than anything else, you have allowed me to become the man and the player that I am today. You made me a father who is blessed with four wonderful children. For all this, I thank you.

Thank you Dominique, Ghislaine, Amandine and Nathan for your unwavering support.

To Micha, who guides me and gives me wise career advice. Thank you!

Aldo and Hakim, you let me experience for the first time all the emotions associated with football. I'll never forget our time at Froges.

Thanks to Bernard Blaquart, Fred Arpinon, Daniel Sanchez, René Girard, Arsène Wenger, Antonio Conte, Maurizio Sarri, Frank Lampard and Didier Deschamps. My football career would not have been the same without your advice, your encouragement and your shouting! Each of you has helped me climb the ladder to success. I know how much I owe you.

My thoughts are with Louis Nicollin, the late chairman of Montpellier Hérault Sport Club and a legend of French football. A lover of the beautiful game, a passionate and engaging man who played a decisive role in my career.

To Anna Stevenson as translator.

Finally, thank you Dominique for helping me to write this book, in which I've truly opened up and shown myself as I am. The unvarnished truth, no filter but all the emotion.

Thanks to Jesus

Thank you, Jesus, for your love.
You give me my inner strength to
always believe.

Amen.

Also available at all good book stores

9781785317927

9781785316470

9781801500067

9781785314995

9781801501286

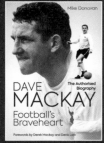

9781785317910

9781785318580

9781785314407

9781785315510